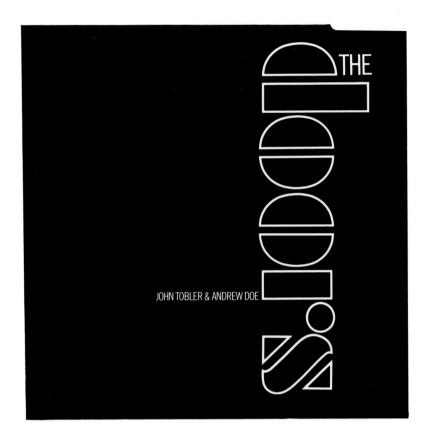

THE DOORS

JOHN TOBLER & ANDREW DOE

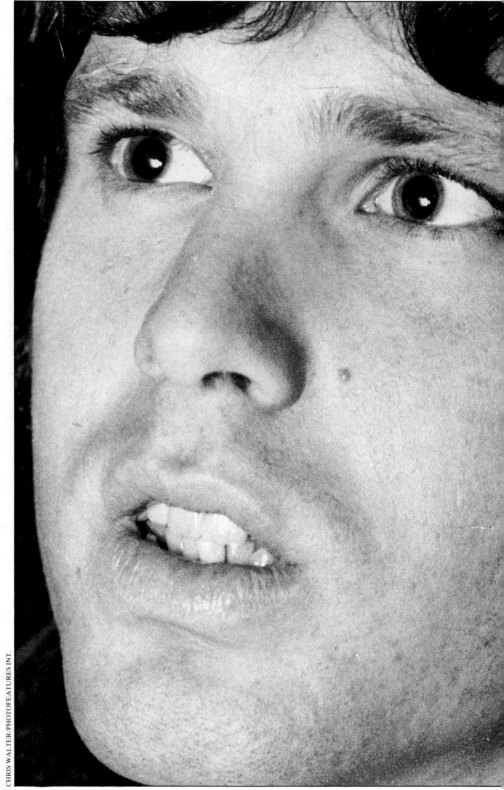

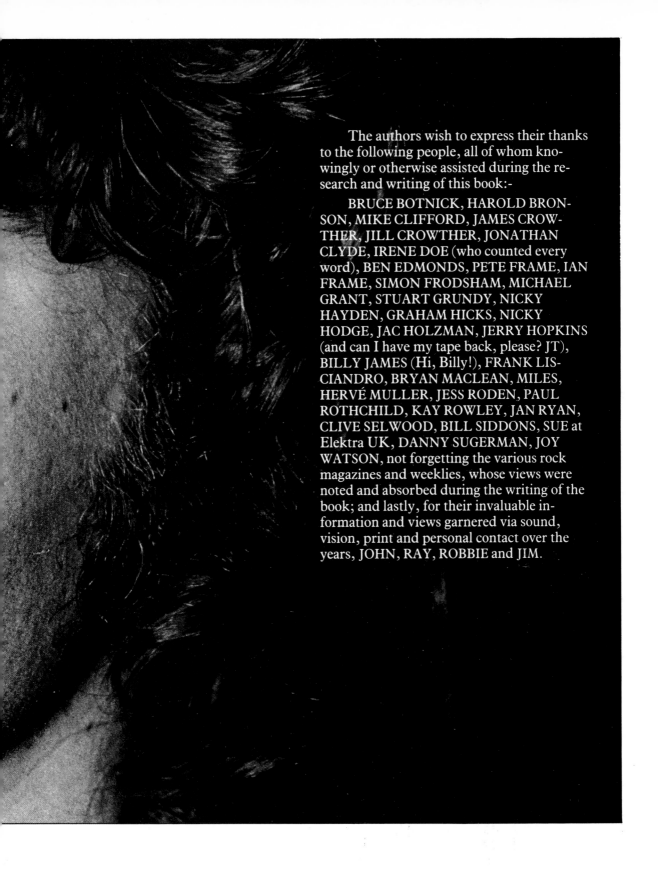

The authors wish to express their thanks to the following people, all of whom knowingly or otherwise assisted during the research and writing of this book:-

BRUCE BOTNICK, HAROLD BRONSON, MIKE CLIFFORD, JAMES CROWTHER, JILL CROWTHER, JONATHAN CLYDE, IRENE DOE (who counted every word), BEN EDMONDS, PETE FRAME, IAN FRAME, SIMON FRODSHAM, MICHAEL GRANT, STUART GRUNDY, NICKY HAYDEN, GRAHAM HICKS, NICKY HODGE, JAC HOLZMAN, JERRY HOPKINS (and can I have my tape back, please? JT), BILLY JAMES (Hi, Billy!), FRANK LISCIANDRO, BRYAN MACLEAN, MILES, HERVÉ MULLER, JESS RODEN, PAUL ROTHCHILD, KAY ROWLEY, JAN RYAN, CLIVE SELWOOD, BILL SIDDONS, SUE at Elektra UK, DANNY SUGERMAN, JOY WATSON, not forgetting the various rock magazines and weeklies, whose views were noted and absorbed during the writing of the book; and lastly, for their invaluable information and views garnered via sound, vision, print and personal contact over the years, JOHN, RAY, ROBBIE and JIM.

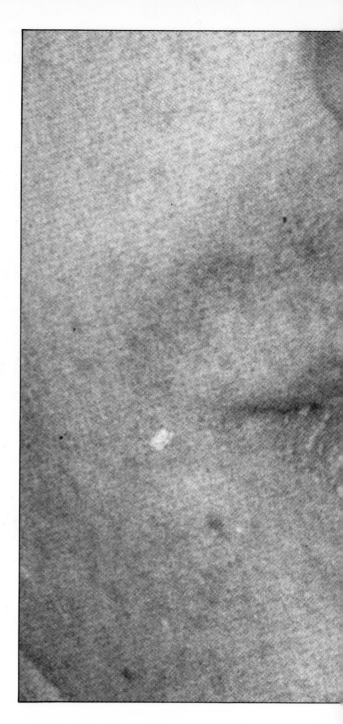

For a figure who was to inspire a fair degree of fear and loathing in the middle America of the mid and late 1960s, the family background and upbringing of James Douglas Morrison was, at first glance, commonplace in the extreme and firmly within the bounds of convention. So much so that, in later years, Jim constantly referred to his parents as both having died, a practice he only discontinued in mid-1969, explaining

"I just didn't want to involve them... I guess I said it as a kind of joke – it's easy enough to find out the personal details if you really want to...".

Whilst such a 'joke' was to become symptomatic of the Morrison persona, Jim's desire not to 'involve' his parents could also be seen as having a slightly more selfish and image-conscious basis, for George Steven Morrison was a career man in the US Navy, a bastion of the very establishment from which Jim sought to free himself.

In later years, Jim's father would attain the exalted rank of Rear-Admiral, but at the time of his eldest son's arrival in this world, he was still rising through the ranks. He had just

transferred from minelaying duties with the

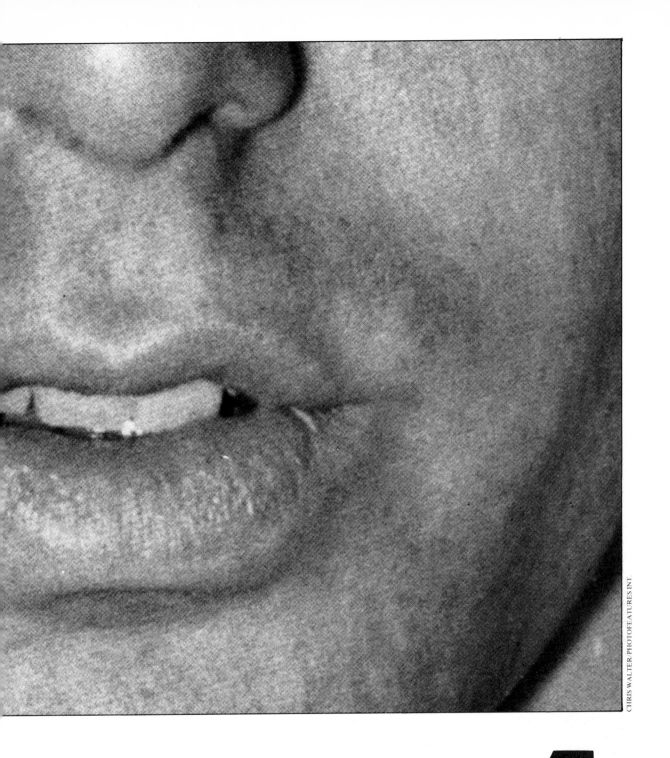

1

Pacific fleet to flight-training in Florida, and it was in the town of Melbourne that Jim was born, on December 8th, 1943. Almost at the same time, his father returned to the Pacific to take part in the slow island-by-island recapture that would take the US forces to the gates of Japan, and the world to the gates of the nuclear age. Thus, for the first three years of his life, Jim and his mother, Clara, lived with Steve Morrison's grandparents, Paul and Caroline Morrison, in Clearwater on the Gulf coast of Florida. Though no-one knew it at the time, this was to be one of the longest settled spells the family Morrison was to experience.

This romany-like existence, criss-crossing the country from base to base, is an accepted part of an officer's life in the armed forces, and is responsible for many, if not most, of Jim's less admirable habits and characteristics. Morrison senior was at best an infrequent resident in the family's varied households during Jim's early life and, it would seem, exercised little parental authority when he was there. In consequence, certain areas of Jim's life lacked discipline, a factor the years failed to rectify.

Upon his father's return from the war in mid-1946, the Morrison family embarked upon its ramblings, spending six months in Washington DC before moving on to Albuquerque, New Mexico, for a year. It was at this latter posting that there occurred what Jim was to come to relate as "the most important moment in my life". Somewhere between Albuquerque and Santa Fe, Jim and his parents were driving along when they came upon a road accident. Jim recalls it as

"The first time I discovered death... Me and my mother and father, and my grandmother and grandfather were driving through the desert at dawn. A truckload of Indians had either hit another car or something – there were Indians scattered all over the highway, bleeding to death. So we pulled the car up... I must have been about four or five and I don't remember if I'd even been to a movie, and suddenly, there were all these redskins, and they're lying all over the road, bleeding to death. I was just a kid, so I had to stay in the car

while my father and grandfather went back to check it out... I didn't see nothing – all I saw was funny red paint and people lying around, but I knew something was happening, because I could dig the vibrations of the people around me, 'cause they're my parents and all, and all of a sudden I realised that they didn't know what was happening any more than I did. That was the first time I tasted fear... and I do think, at that moment, the souls or the ghosts of those dead Indians – maybe one or two of 'em – were just running around, freaking out, and just landed in my soul, and I was like a sponge, ready to just sit there and absorb it... it's not a ghost story, it's something that really means something to me."

Whether Jim used this as a foundation or justification for the later labels of 'shaman' bestowed upon him is now beyond verification, but there can surely be few rock stars who can trace so early an influence with such definition.

In the early months of 1948, Steve Morrison's career took him – and his family – to Los Altos in northern California, where they stayed for almost four years. This period of relative stability was more than compensated for by the following two years, which saw the Morrisons – by now Jim had a sister, Ann and a brother Andrew, respectively three and six years his juniors – move firstly back to Washington DC for a year and then, whilst Morrison senior did his patriotic duty in Korea, back to California, settling for some two years in Claremont, near Los Angeles. Upon his return, the family returned to Albuquerque for a further two years before making tracks back to California and the general area of San Francisco. Slightly over a year later, in December 1958, Jim's father was again posted to Washington and Jim spent the next three years at the George Washington High School there. Ensuring that he became, and remained, the focus of attention of students and tutors alike, he performed a series of stunts calculated to amaze or annoy, depending on one's viewpoint. Similarly, Jim's overall attitude could be seen as idiosyncratic and daring... or that **9**

ROBBIE KRIEGER.

JIM MORRISON.

JOHN DENSMORE

RAY MANZAREK

of a spoilt brat who never seemed to know when to back off, and frequently overstepped the bounds not only of good behaviour, but often of good taste as well. Nonetheless, Jim's grades whilst at school in Alexandria were uniformly high – a fact which doubtless perplexed tutors and classmates alike, as the amount of schoolwork completed was kept to a strict minimum. It was during his High School years that a serious interest in poetry and writing in general first manifested itself:

"I think it was around the 5th or 6th grade, I wrote a poem called Pony Express. *That's the first one I can remember; it was one of those ballad style poems, but I could never get it together. I'd always wanted to write, but figured it'd be no good unless the hand just took hold of the pen and started moving without me really having anything to do with it... but it never happened."*

In addition to poetry, Jim had begun keeping a daily journal, but rather than documenting his mid and late teens, the notebooks were steadily filled with observations, random thoughts and media snapshots that captured his fancy. Any would-be Webermans would doubtless give several vital limbs and functions for the chance to peruse at leisure such valuable texts – and a guided tour of the embryonic adult world of Jim Morrison would illuminate much of what was to follow. But the chance has passed, as Jim explained in a late sixties interview;

"When I left school, for some dumb reason – or maybe it was wise – I threw all those books away, and there's nothing I can think of that I'd rather have in my possession right now than those lost books."

Then, in reflective mood:

"But... maybe if I'd never thrown them away, I'd never have written anything original, 'cause they were mainly things that I had heard or read, like quotes from books... I think if I'd never got rid of them, I'd never have freed myself."

It was during his time in Virginia that Jim also developed a considerable interest in, and affection for, the blues, which combined with his poetic aspirations would in a few years form the basis on which the Doors would operate.

Jim's somewhat-less-than-concerned attitude towards schoolwork extended to embrace a general indifference to his career following graduation. For once, his parents took the initiative, informing him that he was enrolled in St. Petersburg junior college in Florida, and that he would live with his grandparents in Clearwater. Figuring that, at the very least, such an arrangement would afford him expanded personal freedom, Jim acquiesced and in the September of 1961 made the journey to Florida whilst the rest of his family moved on yet again, this time to San Diego, California.

Jim's tenure at St. Petersburg was apparently notable only in that he continued to develop his off-beat behaviour and lifestyle. After a year at junior college, Jim transferred to Florida State University in Tallahassee, initially sharing a house with five fellow students, an arrangement terminated at the end of the first term, by which time Jim had reduced his co-tenants to near breaking point, merely by being Jim. He began the following term living in a small trailer, with no-one but himself to annoy...

Before his second term commenced, Jim had visited his parents in California and caused a considerable stir by announcing his decision to transfer to UCLA to study cinematography. Instead of being relieved at his finally having decided to pursue a definite career, the family Morrison called down a blanket veto on the idea and Jim returned to the FSU. Once there he wasted little time in implementing his planned move, arranging for his grades to be transferred to Los Angeles and taking several courses designed to block in a foundation for the classes at UCLA.

Faced with such a *fait accompli*, Jim's family appeared to relent and allowed him to make the transfer, which he did in the January of 1964. Jim entered the life of the college with relish, and it says much for his still-evolving persona that, even in the often left-field atmosphere of UCLA, he managed to make a mark, by dint of upgraded versions of his earlier antics, mixed for the first time with a dash of drugs and an escalation of his alcoholic intake. Jim formed a small clique with four other would-be film makers, all of whom would have a hand in shaping the Doors, though none so obviously as Dennis Jakob to whom – after a discussion touching on William Blake, Aldous Huxley and their like – Jim proposed the formation of a duo, to be called The Doors: Open and Closed. Setting a pattern that was to become standard during later years, the notion was laid to rest at the talking stage.

Jim had also started to keep a notebook again and, during his days at UCLA, jotted down much of what was to become *The Lords/Notes On Vision*; as he wasn't able to make films yet, writing about them seemed a reasonable substitute

When Jim finally *did* get around to putting a film together, for the final 'exam', such as it was (the course was apparently so liberal that it would have required a concerted effort *not* to graduate), the results were as undisciplined and baffling as anyone who knew him could reasonably expect, and even his staunchest supporters on the teaching staff found their defences finally depleted. Jim, hurt by the attitude of both students and tutors towards his efforts, reacted in typical fashion – he quit UCLA within a few days of the first – and last – screening of what was to be the only film he would ever direct. In many ways, his time at UCLA was generally unproductive, and could have emerged as a complete waste of time, had it not been for a chance meeting with a friend of John de Bella (his cameraman for the untitled film), one Ray Manzarek.

Raymond Daniel Manzarek was born in Chicago on December 2nd, 1939 (or 1942, according to the Elektra biography sheet) and was into music from an early age, though initially with little enthusiasm.

> *"My parents gave me piano lessons when I was around nine or ten, but I hated it for the first four years, until I learned how to do it – then it suddenly became fun. I first heard 'race music', as it was then called, when I was about twelve or thirteen, and from then on I was hooked. Listened to Al Benson, Big Bill Hill – they were disc jockeys in Chicago at the time – and my piano playing changed. I started to be influenced by jazz, learned how to play*

13

UPI

*that stride piano with my left hand, and I
knew that that was it – stuff with a beat.
Jazz, blues, rock...*"

An affection which doubtless caused apoplexy at the Chicago Conservatory, where Ray studied classical techniques for a while.

As an undergraduate to De Paul University, Ray majored in economics and, having obtained his bachelor's degree, headed west to take law at UCLA. After a fortnight it didn't seem such a great idea and he took a post at the Western Bank of America as a management trainee. Three months or so later, he was back at UCLA studying cinematography.

*"At school, I was always interested in
film, as it seemed to combine my interests in
drama, visual arts, music... and the profit
motive!"*

His studies there were continued until December 1961 when, in the throes of a romantic disappointment, he enlisted in the US Army, which seems a remarkably unintelligent thing to have done, even allowing for the emotional stimulus. Ray apparently arrived at the same decision quite rapidly (even though his duties in a Services band in the Orient were hardly onerous) and engineered an early discharge by dint of informing an army psychiatrist he thought he might be developing a severe case of limp wrist. As admitting to being gay was, in those days, on a par with singing the praises of communism, Ray was given his discharge papers a year early, and returned to UCLA to pick up the threads of his film course, coincidentally at the same time as one Jim Morrison arrived from Florida to follow the same syllabus.

With his brothers Rick and Jim and three others, Ray was also pursuing his other love – music. The band was responsible for Jim Morrison's first-ever stage appearance.

*"As Rick and the Ravens, we played
Friday and Saturday nights at the Turkey
Joint West, two blocks from the beach in
Santa Monica. I was in school and it was
like a part-time job... I'd make about $35
a night, which was OK – it paid for the
classes. That was the first time Jim ever
sang on a stage. A whole bunch of guys
from UCLA film school would come*

*down, and there wasn't usually anyone in
the club, so I'd call them all up on stage
and we'd have about twenty guys, singing,
jumping, screaming songs like* Louie
Louie.*"*

Perhaps it was this, or perhaps because he knew Jim through John de Bella, that caused Ray to ask Jim to help him out of a tight corner; Rick and the Ravens were billed to support Sonny and Cher at a graduation hop... but a member had recently quit and Ray needed someone to make up the six musicians stipulated in the contract. The fact that Jim didn't play an instrument was easily glossed over by draping him with a guitar which wasn't even plugged in, much less turned on, and when the show was over, Jim pocketed his fee and disappeared to Venice, Ca., whilst Ray completed his master's degree at UCLA. Jim's splitting to Venice had less to do with any desire to get away from the general environs of UCLA than with his learning that, having lost his student deferment, he'd been classed A-1 at his army physical and was now liable to be drafted. From June to August 1965, Jim lived initially with Dennis Jakob, later on a warehouse roof, ingesting an ever increasing daily ration of LSD, which at that time, in California at least, was both plentiful and legal. It was during this period that the bulk of the songs which the Doors would later record were 'composed'.

*"I was hearing in my head a whole concert
situation, with a band, and an audience –
a large audience. Those first five or six
songs I wrote, I was just really taking notes
at this fantastic rock concert that was going
on inside my head... and once I'd written
these songs, I just had to sing them. The
music came first, and then I'd make up
some words to hang on the melody, because
that was the only way I could remember it,
and most of the time I'd end up with just
the words and forget the tune. I was free
for the first time; I'd been going to school or
college constantly for fifteen years, it was a
beautiful, hot summer, and I just started
hearing songs..."*

In August, Jim's desire to sing those songs took a step nearer to becoming a reality, **15** thanks to a chance meeting with Ray, who not unnaturally still remembers the event with impressive clarity.

> *"A beautiful California summer day, the middle of August, and who should come walking down the beach but Jim Morrison. I said 'Hey man, I thought you were going to New York,' and he said 'Well, I was, but I decided to stay here. I've been at a friend's house, up on his rooftop, writing songs.' I said 'Aha! Why don't you sing one or something?' So what he did was sing* Moonlight Drive... *and when I heard those first four lines, I said 'Wow, that's it – those are the best lyrics I've ever heard for a rock'n'roll song!' As he was singing, I could hear the chord changes and the beat; my fingers immediately started moving. I asked if he had any others, and he said 'Yeah, I've got a lot of 'em', and he went through two or three others, and I said 'Listen, those are the best rock 'n' roll songs I've ever heard – and I've been into music since I was seven years old. Why don't we do something with this?' He said, 'That's what I had in mind. Let's get a rock'n'roll band together' and I said 'Hey, that's a great idea – let's do that and make a million dollars' ...and that's how the Doors got started."*

The name was the least of Ray and Jim's problems in putting the band in motion, as Jim merely disinterred the notion he had proposed to Dennis Jakob.

> *"Jim said, 'How about The Doors?' and I went 'Whaaat? Wait a minute, that's the most ridiculous...no, that's the* best *name I've ever heard for a rock 'n' roll band – The Doors... like the doors of perception', and he said, 'That's it, the doors of perception, the Blake line.' If the doors of perception were cleansed, man could see things as they truly are; infinite. At the time, we had been ingesting a lot of psychedelic chemicals, so the doors of perception were cleansed in our own minds, so we saw music as a vehicle to, in a sense, become proselytisers of a new religion, a religion of self, of each man as God. That was the original idea behind the Doors, using music and Jim's brilliant lyrics."*

Displaying a considerable degree of innate wisdom, Ray decided to devote some time to rehearsing with Jim before introducing the rest of Rick and the Ravens to their new lead singer. To no-one's real surprise, Jim and Rick Manzarek found themselves completely at sea when faced with Morrisonian lyrics, but, to their credit, agreed to give it a go and began rehearsals.

At this point, Rick and the Ravens/proto-Doors consisted of just Jim, Rick & Ray Manzarek (guitar, piano and keyboards & vocals, respectively) and Jim Morrison (vocals and harmonica), the band apparently being in the habit of using any drummer and bassist that came to hand. Ray, however, soon unearthed a drummer, albeit from an unlikely source:

> *"At the time, I was involved with the Maharishi, of Beatle fame, who had just opened a meditation centre on 3rd Street, and in the initial class – you took a series of six lectures before you received your mantra – was John. I'd been talking to one fellow about getting a rock'n'roll band together, and he said 'That guy over there is a drummer'. So I went up to John and said 'Listen man, I'm a keyboard player, and I've got this great singer-songwriter and we're trying to get a band together. We need a drummer – would you be interested?' He said 'Sure, why not?' "*

John Paul Densmore was almost exactly a year Jim's junior, born on December 1st, 1944 in Santa Monica, and had been drumming in one form or another since the age of twelve, leaning more towards jazz as time passed.

> *"I got my first set of drums when I was in junior high. I played sort of symphonic music in High School – tympani, snare – then I played jazz for three years; sessions in Compton and Topanga Canyon",*

which is probably where he joined his first band, Terry Driscoll and the Twilighters, of whom nothing else is known. Prior to the Doors, John drummed for the Psychedelic Rangers, who had recorded one song, *Paranoia Blues*, which has apparently never been released. Initially, John had reservations about joining forces with Ray and Jim;

16

"Their songs were really far-out to me... I didn't understand very much; but then I figured I'm the drummer, not the lyricist."

The band rehearsed for a couple of weeks, then headed for downtown L.A. to cut a demo.

Before Ray had met Jim, Rick and the Ravens had landed a contract with Aura Records, and even managed to release a single (on which Ray was landed with the handle Screaming Ray Daniels!) which, despite – or maybe because of – the promotion Aura afforded, died the proverbial death. Rather than go to the expense of pressing another 45 which would, in all probability, do exactly the same, Aura offered the option of free studio time, an offer Rick and the (new) Ravens/Doors took up. Thus, in September 1965, the band spent three hours at World Pacific Studios on 3rd Street recording six songs which were pressed up into three acetates. The songs were *Moonlight Drive, My Eyes Have Seen You, End Of The Night, Hello, I Love You, Summer's Almost Gone* and *Go Insane* (or *A Little Game*, which Jim would eventually incorporate into *Celebration Of The Lizard*).

Armed with an acetate each, Morrison, Ray and John began doing the rounds of record companies, in the hope of getting a deal. Ray remembers.

"It was funny; in Los Angeles we walked the streets with these demos, went to record companies and said 'Here are six songs, we have many more; listen to these'. And everyone, but everyone, said 'No! You can't – that's terrible – I hate it – no, no'. I especially remember the guy at Liberty. I played him a A Little Game *and said. 'You might like this one'. He listened, then said 'You can't, you can't do that kind of stuff!' Because it said things like 'go insane'. Finally, one guy at Columbia, Billy James, said 'I dig it', and recommended we should be signed up."*

It was round about this time that Jim encountered, and swiftly captivated, Pamela Courson, a nineteen-year old native of Weed, California. This was the beginning of a relationship which came as close to being permanent as was possible where Jim was involved. In the ensuing years, there would

17

be some spectacular rows and separations, but inevitably a reconciliation would be effected – for a while, anyway...

With impeccable timing, Ray's brothers chose this particular moment to call it a day. The loss of Rick on piano was of no great moment, but Jim's guitar was something else. Fortunately, Ray remembered that when he had been recruiting John, the latter had pointed out a fellow meditator as a guitar player.

Robert Alan Krieger, born February 8th, 1946, in Los Angeles, hailed from a musical environment, if not exactly a musical family.

"There was a lot of classical music in my house – in fact, the first music I heard that I liked was Peter & The Wolf. *I think I was about seven. Then... I listened to rock'n'roll on the radio a lot; Fats Domino, Elvis Presley, the Platters. My father liked marching music, and I started playing trumpet at ten, but nothing came of that, so I began playing blues piano – without lessons – then at seventeen, I started playing guitar. Got my own when I was eighteen; it was a Mexican flamenco guitar, and I took flamenco lessons for a few months, until records got me into the blues, the newer rock'n'roll, like Paul Butterfield. If he hadn't gone electric, I probably wouldn't have got into rock 'n' roll. I wanted to learn jazz, really. I got to know some people who did rock'n'roll with jazz, and I thought I would make money playing music".*

Robbie had played with John in the Psychedelic Rangers and was studying psychology at UCLA, "trying to figure out where I was at, actually", when he was asked to join the Doors, as the band had finally become. Ray remembers the first time all four worked together as a magical moment.

"Robbie came down with his guitar and his bottleneck... ah, when he put that big glass bottle on his little finger and went 'boiiinnnggg', I said, 'Whooaa, what a sound! Incredible – that's it, that is the Doors' sound!' The first song we played as a group was Moonlight Drive, *because it didn't have too many difficult chord changes, and after playing that, I said*

'This is it, this is the best musical experience I've ever had'. Of course, we were a little high at the time, but it was just... right, it was right from the beginning. The combination was right, the way John and Robbie and I, with our kind of placid meditation, balanced off Jim's Dionysian tendencies. It was a natural – it couldn't miss. I said, 'This is it, we're gonna make it. We're gonna make great music and the people are going to love it'."

Success, however, wasn't quite as instant as Ray foresaw. The band rehearsed conscientiously all week, did the occasional weekend gig – at which infrequent event, Ray handled most of the vocals whilst Jim stood with his back to the audience, having yet to overcome his unease at performing for someone other than friends – whilst the Columbia contract just lay there and gathered dust. So far, Columbia's support of the band had extended to little more than buying Ray a Vox organ. In December, they began auditioning for various small clubs, in the hope of gaining a residency, but were always turned down for the same reason – no bass player. The dilemma was resolved, ironically, at another failed audition. Ray:

"We auditioned a few bass players, but they didn't have the right personality, or their chops weren't up to snuff, and we thought, what are we going to do about a bass player? Maybe we won't use one at all. But I always felt we had to have somebody on the bottom, because I couldn't get it out of the Vox Continental that I was playing... and it so happened, we auditioned for a gig at some club – we didn't get it, of course – and the house band there had an instrument called a Fender Rhodes piano bass, sitting on top of a Vox organ. I saw that, and I said 'Eureka... I have found it! It sounds like a bass, but you play it like a keyboard...' I had always been trained in a boogie-woogie or stride piano technique, so my left hand always worked independently of my right hand anyway, and when I saw this bass, I knew I could play the bottom with my left hand free to improvise and everything, so the hell with a bass player!"

In January 1966, the Doors finally secured a residency as house band at the London Fog, a somewhat less than salubrious club on Sunset Strip not far from the much more celebrated Whiskey-A-Go-Go. Passing the audition required a fair deal of knavery, as John recalled.

"Actually, how we got in there was, we went down to the audition, and we got about fifty of our friends to pack the place out – because it wasn't a very big place, about forty feet by fifteen – and they all applauded us frantically, and the owner, whose name was Jesse James, thought 'My God!' and hired us. The next night, the place was sort of empty..."

Ray continues the story:

"Nobody ever came in the place... an occasional sailor or two on leave, a few drunks. They had a go-go girl, lovely Rhonda Lane, dancing on the other side... and all in all it was a very depressing experience, but it gave us time to really get the music together. We had to play four or five sets a night; we'd start at nine and play 'til two with fifteen, twenty minute breaks in between and we had the chance to develop songs like Light My Fire, When The Music's Over *and* The End. The End *was originally a very short piece but because of all the time we had to fill onstage, we started extending songs, taking them into areas that we didn't know they would go into... and playing stoned every night. It was the great summer of acid, and we really got into a lot of improvisation, and I think the fact that no-one was at that club really helped us to develop what the Doors became."*

One thing it certainly didn't develop was the communal bank balance. Being a non-union club, the wages at the Fog were breadline at best – $5 during the week and $10 on Fridays and Saturdays... and there was always the very real possibility that the club hadn't taken enough in the preceding week to pay them.

Columbia was of little financial assistance, as Ray recalls:

"We got a couple of amps, and that was about it. Never saw the inside of a

21

recording studio. A guy called Larry Marks came down to the Fog one night and said, 'I'm your producer'… and we never saw him again."

In April, several crises came to a head in swift succession. Jim, who had regained his student deferment from the draft by enrolling at UCLA for classes he had not the slightest intention of taking, was rumbled, reclassified A-1 and told to report in May. The band was dropped by Columbia, a move that John now realises was for the best, although

"At the time we were really depressed at that, but later on, we realised it was great that we got out of that giant company thing, and didn't get lost in the shuffle."

And they were fired from the London Fog, an event which, with hindsight, was the making of the Doors, as Ray explains.

"The owner of the club said 'Listen, you guys, you've been here four months now, and I'm afraid we're gonna have to get a new band' – and we thought, 'God, what are we going to do now?' As the fates would have it, Ronnie Haran, the booking agent for the Whiskey A-Go-Go, came down to hear us, immediately fell in love with Jim, loved the music and asked 'How would you guys like to be the house band at the Whiskey?'. We said, 'Incredible – it so happens we're free. Our engagement here is finished', and we went from making $5 a night to union scale, $135 a week, per man – we felt like we were in heaven! So we played with Them, we played with Love, the Turtles, the Seeds, the Byrds. We were the openers… and Jac Holzman from Elektra Records came down to hear us, and liked the band and finally signed it."

A neatly-packaged summation which glosses over two facts; one, during their three months at the Whiskey, the Doors were sacked, on average, twice a week, either because the owners considered they were playing too loudly (according to John, the general idea was "to blow the headliners off the stage") or, most often, because Jim turned up drunk, stoned, both, or simply didn't turn up. Whenever the firings happened, the band employed a modified version of the con they'd set up to get the gig at the London Fog, namely employing as many of their growing band of fans as they could to inundate the Whiskey with enquiries as to when the Doors were next appearing. It never failed…

One of the headlining acts the band attempted to blow away was Love, and Bryan Maclean remembers the Doors from a time *before* they graduated to the Whiskey.

"They were playing at Sneeky Pete's when we were playing at the Whiskey, and I used to go over there and hang out. And I'd never heard anything quite like it… those four guys. In fact, I wound up living at the Tropicana with Jim, sharing just about everything you could imagine! I didn't like his singing – thought it was horrible – but I was hypnotized by it, amazed by it… something about it caught me."

The other fact is that Jac Holzman reportedly took several visits, not to mention the personal recommendation of Arthur Lee of Love, before he decided to chance his arm and sign the Doors. Somewhat perversely, the band took their time deciding whether or not to accept the offer, consulting Billy James and Ray's father's attorney, Max Fink. Eventually, a deal was struck for a one year contract with an option for two further years, or seven albums, and a producer, Paul A. Rothchild, assigned to them.

"When I first heard them", he recalls, "I wasn't grabbed at all by the Doors. I saw them at a first set at the Whiskey and… it was a pretty bad set; but I stayed for a second set, and they were great, they were incredible."

That Rothchild managed to see the Doors live at all was due to no small amount of luck, for shortly afterwards, the band was finally fired.

Jim missed the first set and when Ray and John dragged him along for the remaining two, he was still well out of it, having reportedly consumed enough acid to blitz the entire population of Hollywood. The second set was, not unnaturally, a mess; the third was apocalyptic. Jim had decided to do their showpiece, *The End*, and Robbie, Ray and John weren't unduly surprised when, about halfway through, some unfamiliar lines made their debut – this was, after all, the nature of the song – and continued the beat as Jim related the killer's awakening, preparation and movements. Anyone with a basic grasp of Greek myths and legends might possibly have had a notion as to what was coming, but such erudition was apparently in short supply at the Whiskey that night.

"Father... Yes, son? I want to kill you / Mother... I want to... FUUCCCKKK YOOUUU!!"

The words were out and Jim was into a familiar section of the song almost before anyone had registered what he'd said. The set finished with the end of the song and the Doors made their way to the artists' back room; here they were confronted by an apoplectic Phil Tanzini, one of the owners, who made it abundantly clear that the services of the Doors in general, and Jim Morrison in particular, were no longer required at his club, with immediate effect.

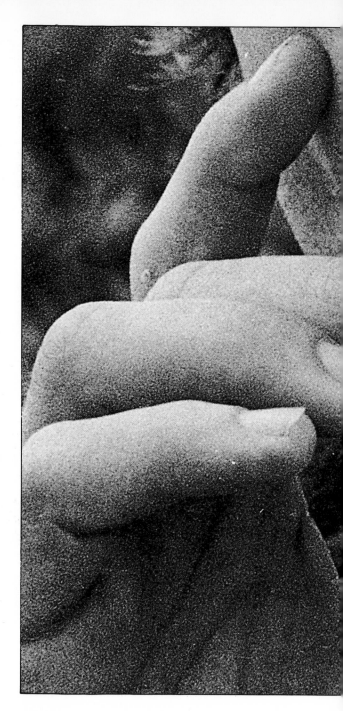

According to Ray Manzarek, the Doors' working relationship with producer Paul A. Rothchild was a

"... a marriage made in heaven. Paul was just what we needed. He came down to the Whiskey a couple of nights and we found him to be a man of like mind, a man who knew his poetry, a man who knew his jazz, rock 'n' roll and folk music and an excellent producer. He was very strong in the studio, and yet he knew enough to give us our heads when we needed to go in our own directions. He never really got in our way... he never really said, 'Well, don't do it that way, do it this way.' Any suggestion he'd have to offer would always be, 'Well listen you guys, what do you think about doing it this way?', and many times his suggestions were correct and we'd say, 'OK, that sounds like a good idea, Paul – let's do it that way.' Paul was an excellent manipulator in the studio."

Rothchild is also to be credited with a fair degree of good timing, for his visit to the Whiskey preceded the Doors' final dismissal from the club by the slender margin of a few days, and had he not witnessed the band live,

24

the ensuing album could well have been a less compelling and less atmospheric artefact.

In the Los Angeles of the mid 1960's, before almost anybody possessed their own recording facilities, four studios reigned supreme, patronised by the likes of such diverse musical talents as Phil Spector, Brian Wilson, the Byrds and Buffalo Springfield. These were Gold Star, Columbia, Western Recorders and Sunset Sound, each having one major scoring point over its rivals. Gold Star, for instance, was generally agreed to have the best echo chamber, whilst at Western, ace engineer Chuck Britz ruled the mixing board. Sunset's claim to fame was its ability to capture or duplicate an open, 'live' feel and Rothchild, having experienced the Doors in concert, decided that it was the sound he wanted for the all-important debut album. Thus it was, in early September, just after the Labour Day weekend, that the Doors and Rothchild booked into Sunset Sound to begin the sessions.

Considering the band's relative inexperience with studio technique – mostly limited to the Aura session or, in Robbie's case, non-existent – recording went very smoothly, due mostly to Rothchild's expertise. He explains:

"The common concept of recording studios – which wasn't mine – was that they were hospitals where the music was operated on. I liked to get as far away from that as possible, convert the atmosphere and emotion of the studio into something warmer... let's sit around and play music for a while – not even, let's sit around in the club and play, because that's also a little alien. So, what we did to break the recording cherry of the Doors, so to speak, was to go into the studio with the band feeling that they're going in for a session. I realised that we'd probably blow a day or so, but we went in to cut masters, not to screw around. We went in and cut two tunes, neither of which showed up on the first album; we didn't stop at a perfect take, we stopped at one we felt had the muse in it. That was the most important thing, for the take to have the feel, even if there were musical errors. When the muse came,that was the take."

One of those initial cuts was the song which had started it all on Venice Beach some twelve months previously, *Moonlight Drive*.

"Actually, that was the first song we recorded," Robbie recalls. *"Probably the reason it wasn't on the first album was because, as it was the first we did, it was probably the worst recorded. So we re-recorded it for the second album... but I still have the tape, the first tape, and it sounds pretty good."*

Another major contributory factor towards the ease with which the sessions unfolded was that the band was exceedingly well rehearsed, and the choice of songs for the album amounted to little more than deciding which numbers worked best live and performing them for Rothchild and engineer Bruce Botnick, whose importance must not be underrated, as Rothchild affirms.

"The engineers are the single most important factor in a studio; just as an artist looks for a creative producer, so will a producer look for a creative engineer. It's that vital – you can have the best studio in the world, but if you've got an inferior engineer, you might just as well have been recording on a portable. Bruce was extraordinarily creative and very pleasant to work with."

Nothing in this world is perfect, however, and the sessions did have their difficult moments. On the musical side, Ray's Fender keyboard bass was proving troublesome.

"It was OK for live work but in a recording studio it just didn't have any definition... a bad sound. It didn't record well and that's why I didn't use it on records any more after that."

Some bass parts were later over-dubbed but largely the tracks were left as they were. The whole album was recorded on 4-track equipment which, in pre-Dolby times, limited the number of overdubs possible before the whole track began to lose definition. Eight tracks did exist – in fact, they'd been around since the late 1950's, pioneered by Tom Dowd at Atlantic – but they were still a rare species in late 1966. Thus the Doors' ability to complete a song in two or three takes, playing the instrumental track in its entirety

26

27

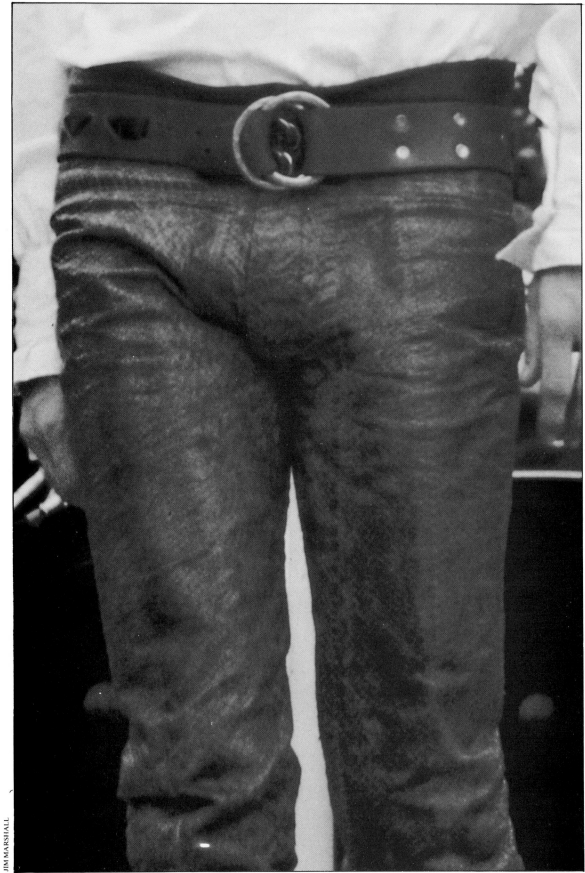

and dubbing the vocals later, proved to be something more than a mere time-saver.

The other problem during the sessions was Jim, or to be more accurate, Jim's increasing consumption of alcohol and drugs. True, *The End* was accomplished in two takes but the preceeding day's session for the track had to be abandoned, courtesy of a generous dose of acid augmented with booze. In the light of future excesses, Jim's intake in 1966 would appear minimal but at the time, it had already become a source of wonder and apprehension.

All but two of the eleven titles eventually included on *The Doors* were originals which had evolved during the band's stints at the London Fog, the Whiskey and other less prestigious gigs. Of the two covers, Robbie remembers

> "I'd heard John Hammond (junior) do Back Door Man, and that's where we got the idea from."

John Densmore adds,

> "Jim liked it a lot,"

which seems quite natural for someone who spent a substantial amount of his high school vacation time in Washington hanging around blues bars. The inclusion of *Alabama Song* rates several interest points on the lyrical content alone, turning out, as it did, to be a reasonably accurate prediction of Jim's future media image. But how did a song from a German opera* find it's way onto a Doors LP, much less their first one? According to Ray,

> "I had a record at home of Brecht/Weill songs and that was just one of them, and we all kind of liked it and said, 'Let's give it a try'."

Paul Rothchild, however, is of the opinion that there was a deeper and more intellectual motive for its inclusion.

> "Both Ray and Jim were admirers of Brecht & Weill for obvious reasons. I suppose they were saying in the Thirties what Jim was trying to get across in the Sixties... in different ways they were both

trying to declare a reality to their generation. The inclusion of Alabama Song *was a sort of a Doors tribute to other brave men in another brave time, even though the lyric is remarkably contemporary. There is another verse which the Doors didn't sing because it was out of context for them. The missing verse is 'Show us the way to the next little dollar/Oh don't ask why', and that wasn't quite what they had in mind."*

Of the originals, all but one had lyrics by Jim set to music by all four... but it must have come as quite a shock to everyone who thought of *Light My Fire* as *the* archetypal Doors (and by association, Jim Morrison) track, to discover that it was largely composed by Robbie who, when questioned about it is suitably modest.

> "Ray had the idea for the opening part, which was the real hook: Jim helped me out on some of the lyrics, too, and the beat was John's idea,"

a disarmingly standard answer which effectively masks the fact that the bulk of the melody and lyric were provided by Mr Krieger! *Light My Fire*, in its complete long form, is a classic Doors song, but in a somewhat different way from the others which were typified by Jim's convoluted wordplays and images; it's a showcase for Ray, Robbie (somewhat less obviously) and John (pretty well imperceptibly). From the driving, classically inspired opening figure to the almost free-form meanderings of the instrumental break occupying the greater portion of the song, Ray displays not only his range of expression but also his tight control; the playing may be loose, but it's never sloppy. Counterpointed for much of the track against Ray's organ is Robbie's guitar, sometimes so slow as to be almost calculated to frustrate, sometimes with the dexterity befitting a flamenco-trained player, always embellishing and adding to the tension. Compared with the exploits of his colleagues, John's part would seem to pale but, as Robbie remarked, it was John who provided the beat and he throws in some unexpected frills and fills.

The bulk of the album, however, *is* Jim Morrison, lyrically and, despite what the **31**

---

*Bertolt Brecht & Kurt Weill co-wrote *The Threepenny Opera* in 1928 and on more than one occasion, the Doors would also include *Mack The Knife* (the most familiar song from the 'opera') in live performances.

sleeve may say, musically. Jim's lyrics are one of the cornerstones of the Doors' legend/ myth, nurtured and reinforced over the years almost to a point beyond criticism or, indeed, further comment. To the casual rock observer, the man dispensed polished gems in every song he concocted... so what is the newcomer to the music of the Doors to make of such tracks as *I Looked At You* or *Take It As It Comes*? Again, Paul Rothchild provides the answer;

> *"Those represent, probably more than any other songs, the genesis of the group. They were the earliest songs on the album; the later tunes were deeper, show a greater maturity."*

By 'later', one assumes Rothchild means recorded as opposed to composed and such maturity is especially evident in *Soul Kitchen*, one of a batch of song-poems dating back to Jim's residency on a Venice warehouse roof. On the surface, it's a simple tribute to a restaurant Jim had frequented... until the couplet "your fingers weave quick minarets/ speak in secret alphabets" unexpectedly jumps out of the fabric of the song, a flash of brilliant imagery which immediately alters the entire meaning of the song, crystallising a theme tentatively stated in *Break On Through* and one which was to be continued and expanded throughout the album. *End Of The Night* is another so-so lyric redeemed by a suddenly memorable twist ("some are born to sweet delight/some are born to the endless night/end of the night") and is also an interesting example of a song in the making. A year or so later, it would appear in its final form as *When The Music's Over*, the Doors' second 'epic' track and successor to the apocalyptic *The End*.

Until *A Day In The Life* from the Beatles' *Sgt. Pepper* came along a few months later, *The End* was adjudged as one of the most – if not *the* most – controversial, celebrated and analysed album tracks to emerge from rock-'n'roll. Its capture on vinyl was always representational and never intended as final, as Rothchild explains.

> *"The End was always a changing piece. Jim tended to use it as a kind of open, almost blank canvas for his poetic bits and pieces, images and fragments, couplets and the little things he just wanted to say, and it changed all the time, it was always a fluid situation. After it was down on record, they could listen to it and tended to perform it that way, but Jim still used to leave something out, put something else in, transpose verses."*

Certainly anyone who remembered the original simple two verse love song could affirm that over the months the piece had not only grown in length but also in complexity and stature. The recorded version, complete with the Oedipal segment, had only been performed once prior to recording – at the Whiskey, some eleven minutes before the Doors were given their cards once and for all – so its appearance on the record in this full form was at once anticipated yet unexpected. As to what it meant precisely, the listener was left to draw his own conclusions assisted by Jim's clues and signposts. Paul Rothchild saw it this way:

> *"Jim was fascinated with the concept of death, spiritual death rather than physical death; it's a theme of many of his songs. I'm not sure if this is what Jim had in mind – I never asked him, he just presented it to me and said, 'Interpret it as you will' – but it's as if Jim is saying as a friend "This is the end, my friend," and so on. The line 'the nights we tried to die' is, to me, a direct reference to the theory that most mind-expanding drugs are actually a form of physical poisoning, a means of re-orienting the body by poison. The trip has started and it's the end, because every time we take a trip, there's death, a death of concepts and bullshit, of laughter and soft lies... and with every end there is a beginning. Things are very wrong out there, so let us kill those things in ourselves which are false: 'Can you picture what will be/so limitless and free/desperately in need of some stranger's hand/in a desperate land?' The other imagery in the song, those little poetic parts between the original first and last verses, is Jim just saying, 'Get down to reality'. The snake thing is just pure sexual imagery, of course, it comes right out of the blues imagery which Jim was very familiar*

with. What he was saying was that there were few realities in life and that one of the few truly 'real' realities is sexual companionship and awareness...Jim was very lucid in that department.' Lost in a Roman wilderness of pain'– a beautiful piece of classical imagery, great crumbling ruins of a mighty civilisation, which of course related to what was going on then... 'And all the children are insane/waiting for the summer rain'; insanity is another form of symbolic death, and the cleansing, the summer rain, is a rebirth. And then there's that amazing Oedipal section, the first big build. Jim screamed there, for obvious reasons, because even for him there were cultural strictures... but it's more effective, basic, primal, the reason and the motivation. What he was basically suggesting at the end of that section was that we should kill the alien concepts, get back to reality; and that's what the song is all about – the end of alien concepts and the beginning, the rebirth of personal concepts. Discover, search for your own reality."

An impressive dissertation; however, Rothchild freely admits to the possibilities of less esoteric and literary influences on the recording:

"I'm reasonably sure that Jim was still on an acid trip, but it was done during the after-period, the clear light, the reflective part of a trip."

The producing and engineering of *The End*, as recounted by Rothchild, was pretty much a trip in its own way.

"That half hour when we recorded The End *was one of the most beautiful moments I've ever had in a recording studio. I was totally overwhelmed. Normally, the producer sits there just listening for all the things that are right and anything about to go wrong, but for this take I was completely sucked up into it, absolutely audience. The studio was completely dark except for a candle in Jim's booth and the VU meters on the mixing board; all the other lights were off, it was a magic moment, and it was almost a shock when the song was over. It was like, yeah,* that's the end, that's the statement – *it can't go any*

further. There were about four other people in the control room, and we realised the tapes were still rolling, because Bruce, the engineer, was also completely sucked into it. His head was on the console and he was just absolutely immersed in the take – he became audience too... so the muse did visit the studio that time, and all of us were audience; the machines knew what to do, I guess..."

Fortunately, not all the sessions were that intense and the album was recorded in the remarkably short time of two weeks. A further five weeks were required for mixing, after which the Doors flew to New York on a two-fold mission, firstly to unveil their music for the first time outside their home town which they duly did to great acclaim at Ondine's in Manhattan, and also to finalise arrangements with Elektra over publishing and promotion of the album. It was decided that a single, *Break On Through*, would be released at the same time and Jac Holzman, ever mindful of the restrictive nature of playlists and the extreme moral sensibilities of programmers, insisted that the word 'high' be edited from the song's middle-eight. These days, having one's debut 45 banned is supposedly guaranteed to ensure a chart placing, but back in 1967 it was a different matter altogether. Reluctantly, the band acquiesced, hence the somewhat puzzling repetition of "she get/she get/she get".

Both the album, entitled simply *The Doors*, and the single were scheduled for a January 1967 release and Elektra were sufficiently impressed with the product to bring as much promotional muscle to bear as they could. The campaign included the first-ever rock billboard to be seen overlooking Sunset Strip in Hollywood – bearing the catch-all phrase "The Doors Break On Through With An Electrifying Album". The board also bore a sleeve shot from the album, though interestingly, it was the back sleeve photo, in which Jim almost disappears between Ray and Robbie. The front slick, on the other hand, told the world what LA nightclubbers already knew – that the Doors effectively equated with Jim Morrison and three others, Jim's 'artistic' head-shot forcing Ray, Robbie

& John to crowd together on the left-hand side.

The Doors is one of the most stunning debut albums in the history of rock, turning accepted maxims upside down. Here, instead of foundations being laid for later construction, the best came first. Rothchild's decision to use Sunset Sound paid handsome dividends for the overwhelming impression on first hearing is, 'Where is the audience?' – the 'live' feel is genuinely that intense and intense is the keyword. Given the unusual instrumentation, the depth and mood attained is astonishing and the power remains as forceful today as it was then. What really set it apart from almost any other album of 1967 was that it *was* apart from pretty well every vein of mainstream rock. Certainly Jim's youthful assimilation of the blues is evident to a greater or lesser degree on most tracks and there is a hint of the Kinks sound which would reappear in later years but the whole is something else altogether.

The Doors were operating in a foreign land with the Velvet Underground as their only fellow travellers. At the dawn of a year which would spawn the so-called "Summer of Love", the Doors presented another, darker aspect of the same scene already synthesised by the Beach Boys and due to be immortalised by the Beatles, a time of good vibrations when all that was needed was love. Ray, partially quoting Jim, summed up the whole Doors ethos, and in particular their early albums, when he said

"There are things you know about, and things you don't – the known and the unknown – and in between are the doors: that's us. We're saying that you're not only spirit, you're also this very sensuous being. That's not evil, that's really a beautiful thing. Hell appears so much more fascinating and bizarre than heaven. You have to 'break on through to the other side' to become the whole being."

Strange words from a practitioner of Transcendental Meditation... Jim added a qualifying rider;

"We are from the west. The world we suggest should be a new wild west, a

sensuous, evil world, strange and haunting."

The timing of *The Doors* was, whether by accident or design, exceedingly fortuitous; there were no real competitors. Love had never really achieved the public recognition their peers thought they deserved whilst everybody else, it seemed, was gearing up for the summer, little knowing what Messrs Lennon and McCartney were concocting in Abbey Road's studio No. 2. For the time being, however, the Doors were 'where it was at', even if none of the reviewers of the album were quite sure where 'it' was. Ray, looking back, gives his view;

"The first album was an existential album. It's four incredibly hungry young men, striving and dying to make it, desperately wanting to get a record, a good record, out to the American public and wanting the public to like the record. I think any artist wants the public to like his act, or his record; I think that any artist creates from a driving inner need, but there's this outer need that's very important too, and that's acceptance by some people, somewhere, somehow… someone saying to you, 'I like the work you've created.' That's what being an artist is. So The Doors *was that incredible, existential first time – 'Here they are, first time out, fresh, brand new and hungry as hell !!'"*

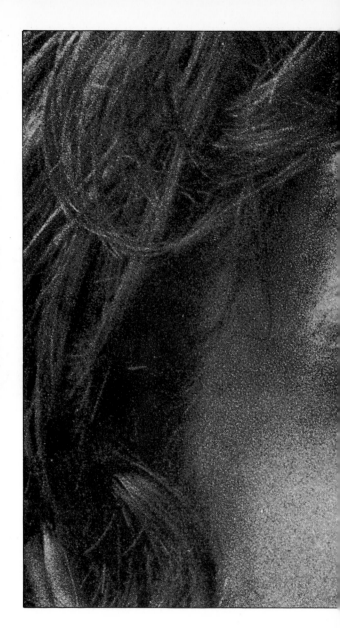

If the reviewers found themselves some-what at sea in their attempts to come to terms with The Doors (perversely, most of them chose to concentrate on the most complex track, *The End*, with such phrases as "Joy-cean stream-of-consciousness pop" and "Dionysian word drama" cropping up) or, indeed, the band as an entity, the teen magazine editors viewed the band – or rather Jim – as a gift from the Gods. Here was an articulate, intelligent artist who provided not only good copy laced with quotes heavy with erudition and vague menace, but also sported the most photogenic features since Elvis Presley. Thus Jim's early media image, as far as those outside looking in were concerned, was almost schizoid in its extremes. On one hand, the "erotic politician, interested in anything about revolt, disorder, chaos, espe-cially activity that seems to have no meaning" and on the other, object of school-girl fanta-sies, soon to be thumbtacked to bedroom walls all over America.

This, however, was as yet a concern of the near-future – of more pressing import was the promotion of *The Doors* and *Break On Through* by means of personal appearances.

In the same month as the LP and single were released, the band played the Fillmore Auditorium in San Francisco, at that time the premier "underground" emergent rock venue, and stole the show from Sopwith Camel and the Young Rascals, a feat they repeated some weeks later on their return, this time upstaging San Francisco's favourite sons, the Grateful Dead. So rapidly did a Doors' following evolve in the Bay area that, upon their third visit in mid-March, the band played their first major headlining concert at the Avalon Ballroom. Sandwiched between these jaunts to northern California were numerous hometown gigs, pushing the single to the fringes of the Los Angeles top ten. This was an encouraging response for a debut 45 – even for a hometown band – but *Break On Through* signally failed to make any impact on the national charts. The album fared rather better, entering the lists in the last week of March, doubtless boosted by a second successful week-long engagement at New York's Ondine's.

Back in Los Angeles, the Doors returned to the studio. On the strength of public reaction, it had been decided to release *Light My Fire* as the second single, but its inordinate length caused a few problems. After considering a "part 1 / part 2" type release, the band eventually agreed to cut a new, shorter version. The attempt proved abortive and the single released in April was the album cut with a large section of the climactic instrumental break excised by Paul Rothchild. John Densmore explains:

"We always made an album as an album; we never really tried to make singles. We'd make the album, then after it was mixed we'd sit back when it was possible to be more objective, and then we might think, 'OK, what might be commercial for AM airplay?'. We'd accept a little feedback from the record company on that, because having an AM single promotes the album and you want to have people hear the album…".

The emasculated *Light My Fire* was released in April and, rather surprisingly considering it was something of a 'public demand'

release, it hung around for several weeks doing nothing nationally.

The Doors, in contrast, were as busy as they'd ever been, undertaking their first headlining appearance at the Fillmore in June before flying to New York once more for a successful three-week residency at The Scene, despite the fact that the club closed for the three days of the Monterey Pop festival. That the Doors, a band from Los Angeles, should be overlooked when this ground-breaking event was conceived, appears to be something of a slight but the fact is that when the festival was first mooted, they were indeed just another band from L.A. Nonetheless, they were less than pleased at being excluded.

However, both the single and the LP were making determined progress up the national charts and, after a hesitant start, *Light My Fire* broke into the top 100 in early June and climbed steadily until it reached number one during the last week of July. Doubtless boosted by the performance of the single, the album (which had entered the charts in late March) rose to number two and would surely have made number one had not the Beatles released *Sgt. Pepper's Lonely Hearts Club Band*. As it was, *The Doors* spent over two years in the charts.

Still riding the high of (almost) topping both major sales charts, the Doors returned to Sunset Sound to commence recording their second album, again produced by Paul Rothchild and engineered by Bruce Botnick. The room in which they had recorded *The Doors* was unchanged, but technology had taken several significant steps forward. Ray:

"Strange Days is when we began to experiment with the studio itself, as an instrument to be played. It was now 8-track and we thought, 'My goodness, how amazing! We can do all kinds of things – we can do overdubs, we can do this, we can do that… we've got eight tracks to play with!' It seems like nothing today, in these times of thirty-two or even forty-eight track recording, but those eight tracks to us were really liberating. So, at that point, we began to play… it became

39

five people; keyboards, drums, guitar, vocalist and studio".

The most obvious example of pure studio technique occurs in *Horse Latitudes*, a resurrected highschool poem written by Jim. The basic track of wind-like sound was obtained by a "white noise" tape being hand-wound, over which was dubbed a cacophony of randomly played instruments and Jim's semi-histrionic incantation. In 1967, Jim explained it thus;

"It's about the Doldrums where sailing ships from Spain would get stuck. In order to lighten the vessel, they had to throw things overboard; their major cargo was working horses for the New World, and this song is about that moment when the horse is in the air. I imagine it must have been hard to get them over the side, 'cause when they got to the edge, they probably started chucking and kicking... and it must have been hell for the men to watch, too, because horses can swim for a while, but then they lose their strength and just go down... slowly sink away."

Other examples of studio experimentation crop up throughout the album. On the title track, for instance, Jim's vocals are echoed by a primitive synthesizer tone, and although somewhat less than an unqualified success as it renders Jim comparatively indistinct without some effort on the part of the listener, it certainly adds to the mystic atmosphere of the piece. A more successful idea was to record John's cymbal track in *I Can't See Your Face In My Mind* backwards, presumably at Rothchild's instigation. Ray remembers another of his ideas for that particular track;

"We were having trouble getting the song. We tried it three or four times and then Paul came in and said, 'Alright, now everybody sit down'. He lit a candle, lit some incense in the studio and said, 'I want you guys all to feel that you're in Japan. Think of a Japanese koto [an instrument similar to a dulcimer], think of a geisha house, think of a warm bath in Japan... get into this mood, think of being very relaxed and very oriental' and, in effect, he hypnotised us – did a beautiful job. His

voice had a low, rolling quality to it, and he set this mood that was so perfect that it took just two takes to get the song, and it was exactly the way the song was supposed to be."

This time round, all the tracks were Doors' originals with Robbie supplying the lyrics to *Love Me Two Times* and *You're Lost Little Girl*, and Jim the remainder. The music was the usual collaboration. Mindful of the problems Ray's keyboard bass had posed during the sessions for the first album, Doug Lubahn, then of fellow Elektra group Clear Light, was drafted in, the first of a succession of studio bass players over the years.

In September, whilst the sessions for the album were still underway, the band released *People Are Strange* as a preview of the new LP, a practice which was to become standard Doors' procedure. With more than a passing musical nod in the direction of *Alabama Song*, the song was nonetheless firmly in the established Doors groove and, doubtless riding on the success of *Light My Fire* (still lodged high in the charts), rose quite swiftly to number twelve.

The following month, *Strange Days* made its appearance and, if the bizarre circus procession on the sleeve of midgets, acrobats, a juggler and a transvestite strongman (– and it's rumoured that the model in the doorway on the back cover is Karen Astley, now Mrs. Pete Townshend) gave reviewers pause for thought, the music within reassured. The Doors were still pursuing their own idiosyncratic vision of a present where perhaps not everything was as peaceful and beautiful as the prevailing trend of rock would have the audiences believe. *Moonlight Drive* was a simple – if Morrisonesque – tale of life at Venice Beach until the single line "gonna *drown* tonight" twists everything back on itself. The title track established the mood for the whole set, a nebulous affirmation of vague menace, whilst the very titles of *You're Lost Little Girl* and *Unhappy Girl* betray their preoccupation with the alienation that was the other face of the Summer of Love... and the songs, perhaps obtusely, expressed Jim's dawning emotions regarding the rock business.

41

JIM MARSHALL

The centrepiece of the album was the Doors' first overtly political statement, *When The Music's Over*. In the same way as *The End*, it appears to have developed from a relatively simple and much shorter song (*End Of The Night*, perhaps, from the previous album?) into an expansive catalogue of accusations, observations, instructions and demands, climaxing inexorably with "we want the world and we want it NOW!" In many ways, the track is superior to *The End*, especially regarding the performances of John and Robbie who are equally excellent throughout the album. But, as is the case with the whole album, there's a nagging feeling that something isn't quite as it should be, that perhaps the incredible rush of that remarkable debut was waning or it had been something of a flash in the pan.

Both assumptions are, to a greater or lesser

degree, valid. As Ray said, the first LP was four hungry guys wanting to get a record out come hell or high water, and of course, there was no way that such an atmosphere could carry over to a second disc recorded some six months later. Also, although both albums comprised material which the Doors had been performing live for some time, the better material had inevitably been used for the initial release. That isn't to say that the songs on *Strange Days* were in any way sub-standard, just that, in comparing their impact, they appeared slightly second best.

For its time, and even today, *Strange Days* was and is an excellently executed and produced record and contained innovations previously considered the exclusive preserve of the Beatles (who, by the way, were still using 4-track equipment at the time), notably one of the earliest uses of a synthesizer by a

major rock band, pre-dated only by the Beach Boys and, amazingly, the Monkees!

Whatever the critics thought of the album, the fans considered it good enough to push to the number three spot in the national charts within two months of its release, and to keep it there for just over a year, due in no small part to the group's constant touring throughout America and the growing cult of Jim Morrison. Descriptions of Doors gigs as rituals with Jim as the presiding shaman were beginning to appear, no doubt causing confusion amongst fans who had just gone along for a good time. Ray considers that these views were valid, nonetheless;

> "*Jim Morrison as Dionysus, a Greek god reincarnate. Apollo was the god of light, clear thought, logical thinking; Dionysus was the god of feeling, internal feelings, a god of spontaneity, the dance, the music. Dionysus enters the body through the ears, through music, through primitive rhythms, and Jim was Dionysus personified. The man onstage was an absolute genius, a human theatricon; from one performance to the next, you never knew what he was going to be. Sometimes a devil, sometimes a saint. Sometimes an angel, sometimes a demon from Hell, the Banshee himself. I've never seen a performer like Jim – it was as if it wasn't Jim performing, but a shaman. Traditionally, a shaman was a man of the tribe who would go on a voyage in his mind, who would let his astral body project out into space and, in a sense, heal the tribe and find things that were needed for the safety of the tribe, for the continuance of the species. So, in a modern sense, Jim was exactly the same thing. Jim always said, 'We may never do this again, so let's do it for real, right here and now on this stage, because if we don't do it now, we may never have the opportunity again. The future is uncertain, the end is always near and if we don't do it now... if we don't get in touch with the gods, with our own feelings, our own spirituality, then we've lost this golden opportunity, this moment in reality that will never come again'. Jim was always very aware of the fact that each moment was precious, a*

jewel, a drop in time, and it's all we had. We had the present – we didn't have the past, we didn't have the future – and when the Doors stepped on stage, all there was was the present. This holy moment; four guys on stage, an audience out there and the energy flowing back and forth between them in what became, in a sense, a communion. My energy had been totally spent, and I felt cleansed of any evil and darkness. We walked out of a concert feeling absolutely in touch with the universe, and that, if any, was the message of Jim Morrison: 'Get in touch with yourself. When you do that, you'll be in touch with God, you become *gods...' Jim's message was that everyman is a god – all you have to do is realise it."*

John Densmore confirms that a Doors concert was an 'event', as much for the band as it was for the audience:

"It was total threatre – it wasn't planned or conceived in the studio, it was fairly subconsious. Jim was magical – he never quite knew what he was going to do each night, and that's what was so exciting – the suspense, because obviously we didn't really know either. Our framework was our music, but it didn't seem that rigid; somehow we could go off on a tangent for twenty minutes or so, and Jim would stretch out, improvise some poetry and we'd vamp along, comment on his poetry and improvise for a while, then we'd get back into the chorus of the song... so that was what made it so exciting. Plus he had a great rapport with the audience; he could really work 'em up!"

Audiences, it appeared, were not the only things Jim could 'work up'. In the fall of 1967, the Doors appeared on the Ed Sullivan Show. There was just one small problem; CBS vetoed the use of the word 'higher' in their performance of *Light My Fire* and the band were requested to substitute another line, which they readily agreed to. Needless to say, the original line was reinstated during the live broadcast and all hell was let loose in the control room. In itself, it seemed a small point but, in the light of events to come, indicated the source of the media's distrust of the Doors in general and Jim in particular, and the Doors' disdain for convention and the false moral values imposed by people whom they considered completely out of touch.

By November, the Doors were America's number one press darlings, discussed and analysed in the pages of such diverse publications as *Time, Life, Vogue* and *16*. The majority of the later-to-become 'classic' Morrison quotes date from this period, for example,

"I think the highest and the lowest points are the important ones; all the points in between are, well, in between. I want freedom to try everything – I guess I want to experience everything at least once."

One thing Jim had experienced considerably more than once, and something which began to play an increasing role in both his and the Doors' history from roughly this time onwards, was alcohol and it began replacing acid and other hallucinogenics as his main escape route. Jim had once explained to a friend,

"I can gauge it so that I can tell, I can stay in one place. Every sip is another chance... another chance at bliss."

Evidently the gauge was faulty one November night when the Doors played Bill Graham's Winterland with Jim as satisfactorily drunk as anyone had ever seen him, at least in public.

Nineteen-sixty-seven had been such a successful year for the Doors – two top five albums, three top thirty singles (*Love Me Two Times*, released in November, peaked at twenty-five) and the added bonus of *Light My Fire* and *The Doors* achieving gold disc status within days of each other – that it was not too far removed from tragic, yet somehow inevitable, when the lines were finally crossed in New Haven, Connecticut, on the day after Jim's twenty-fourth birthday. The previous night at a gig in Troy, New York, the audience had been less than demonstrative, even to the point of denying the group an encore. The New Haven crowd was more responsive, the gig was a good, average Doors concert... until the last song, *Back Door Man*. During the instrumental break, **45**

Jim began intoning to the rhythm of the music and the audience quickly grasped that this was something apart from the usual Morrison improvisation.

"I want to tell you about something that happened just a few minutes ago right here in New Haven..."

Jim related his activities that evening, dinner, people he'd talked with, arriving at the venue, meeting a girl backstage...

"and we started talking, and we wanted some privacy, so we went into the shower-room. We were not doing anything, you know, just standing there and talking... and then this little man came up, this little man in a little blue suit and a little blue cap... and he said 'Whatcha doin' there?' 'Nothin'' ... but he did not go away. He stood there and then he reached around behind him and brought out this little can of something... looked like shaving cream... and then he sprayed it into my eyes – I was blinded for about 30 minutes!!!"

at which point he swung straight back into the song – for about thirty seconds, because that was how long it took to switch on the auditorium lights. As Jim was alternately asking the crowd if they wanted more music and shouting "Turn off the lights!", police officers arrested him, despite the efforts of Bill Siddons, the Doors' road manager. During the ensuing struggle to get Jim off stage and into a squad car, two reporters and a photographer from *Life*, newly returned from Vietnam, were also arrested. At the police station, Jim was charged with breach of the peace, giving an indecent and immoral exhibition and resisting arrest and placed under a $1500 bond, which Bill Siddons covered from the concert receipts.

What had actually happened was substantially what Jim had described onstage; the police were clearing the backstage area of hangers-on and one of the officers had not recognised Jim and told him and the girl he was with to move out. Whether through devilment or annoyance at not being recognised, Jim had apparently taunted the cop and was duly maced with the 'little can of something' (mace is the common name for a

form of aerosol tear gas, sprayed directly into the victim's face). As far as can be ascertained, no charges were ever actually brought to bear, but the incident further soured Jim's already almost non-existent respect for the forces of law and order, as well as simultaneously confirming the growing suspicions the 'establishment' had about the Doors, and adding to the band's hip quotient.

The early weeks of 1968 were equally inauspicious, as the band went back into Sunset Sound to begin recording the next album. The basic problem, Robbie explains,

"was the 'third-album syndrome'. Usually a group will have enough songs in their repertoire to record one, or maybe two albums, and then what'll happen is they go on tour and they don't have time to write any more stuff, so by the third album, you find yourself trying to write stuff in the studio, and it shows, usually."

The Doors initially thought they had this angle covered, for one side of the LP was slated to be occupied by Jim's epic recitation, *Celebration Of The Lizard*, a composition which, in the manner of *The End*, had been evolving for many months – in fact, a section of it was recorded on the very first proto-Doors demo – whilst during the latter months of 1967, Jim had been coming up with some of his most political songs to date, among them *The Unknown Soldier*. But almost from the beginning, the sessions began to go wrong, their shortcomings being almost entirely due to Jim, who took to inviting friends and assorted hangers-on to the sessions, then proceeded to drink himself into a stupor. Things got to such a pitch that one night John threw his drumsticks across the studio and announced that enough was enough.

"It was the third album syndrome... I was just frustrated. On a couple of nights, I felt... I was just hinting that I was dissatisfied, wanting to drop out, whatever. Maybe I was trying to say to Jim, don't be so self destructive..."

He was back for the next day's session, but it was obvious that something would have to be done or there might never be a third album. Rothchild came up with the suggestion of hiring Bob Dylan's ex-roadie/minder, Bobby Neuwirth (now a respected musician in his own right). The other three agreed and Elektra, having been appraised of the situation, also agreed and went so far as to contribute towards the cost of engaging him. Ostensibly, Neuwirth was to direct a film documentary on the band, but there is little doubt that Morrison knew exactly what was going on.

As if the Doors didn't already have enough trouble, they chose this particular moment to reshuffle their management. The prevailing feeling was that, efficient as Dann & Bonafede (who had managed the group since the signing of the record contract with Elektra) had been, their increasing pressure on Jim to break from the band and go it alone was hardly in the best interests of the group. Their replacement was Bill Siddons, promoted from road manager.

The band could now re-focus its attention on the album, which was proving ever more troublesome. By March, two cuts, one being *The Unknown Soldier*, were finished and released as a single, accompanied by a promotional film. However, the content of the song and the film effectively prevented it from getting any worthwhile airplay or TV exposure and it only just scraped into the top forty. Meanwhile, a much bigger problem occupied the band's mind back in the studio; *Celebration Of The Lizard* just wasn't working. Over various sessions, all the elements had been recorded and roughly edited into a version lasting just under twenty five minutes, but only Jim was happy with it. The other Doors and Rothchild considered the track too inaccessible to warrant further precious studio time and it was accordingly dropped from the album, except for the most musically acceptable section, *Not To Touch The Earth*.

To fill the sudden void, the band turned to the few remaining songs from Jim's Venice period and were also forced to come up with new, studio-written material. Similarly, arrangements had to be worked out on the spot for some songs, as opposed to their being worked up in concert. This general feeling of uncertainty was reflected in the

multiple takes that almost all the songs required. Jim had become bored. The initial thrill of being a media idol had worn off and was replaced by annoyance that his original concept for the Doors was being pushed aside by its new public image. Coupled with his disappointment at the fate of *Celebration Of The Lizard*, it's not surprising that he returned to his previous preoccupations, film and poetry.

As the album sessions limped to a close in May, it was decided to shoot a full-length documentary of the Doors, on and off stage. Bobby Neuwirth having recently departed the scene, two former UCLA friends of Jim & Ray were hired to shoot, edit and direct the movie; they were Frank Lisciandro and Paul Ferrera, the latter adding an old school friend of his own to the team, 'Babe' Hill, destined to become one of Jim's closest friends. Despite the generally negative response to *Celebration Of The Lizard*, he was pleased with it and began making serious moves to have his poetry published.

In the meantime, the band was still touring, but Jim was becoming more and more disillusioned, to the extent that, at a Chicago show on May 10th, 1968, he successfully managed to incite the crowd to riot and the fans stormed the stage after the second encore.

The second preview single from the new album, *Hello, I Love You*, was released in early June and, although it possibly caused a few hardline fans some anguish, it reached number one and provided the band with its first UK hit of any substance. Not long after its release, Jim staggered everyone by walking into the Doors' offices one day and announcing he was leaving the group because it wasn't what he wanted to do anymore. As with John's similar announcement during the album sessions, nothing came of it, but that he had even considered such a move was evidence of his growing disillusionment.

Waiting For The Sun (previously entitled *Celebration Of The Lizard*), was released in July 1968 and, surprisingly, also reached number one in the charts. Surprisingly because, compared with the two preceding albums, it was a patchy, almost schizoid disc,

requiring minimal detective work to separate the songs of earlier vintage from those hurriedly composed as 'fillers'. The latter shared two shortcomings – banal lyrics and lacklustre vocals from Jim. *Summer's Almost Gone*, *Wintertime Love* and *Yes, The River Knows* were Doors songs only by virtue of being performed by the band. *We Could Be So Good Together* and *Spanish Caravan* at least boasted the respective merits of some interesting word play and an inspired adaptation of a flamenco guitar piece. Strangely, one of the 'instant' songs worked amazingly well, the *a capella* arrangement, execution and sound effects of *My Wild Love* conjuring a picture of Jim thinking, "OK, they're calling me a shaman; let's give 'em a shaman's chant!"

Very few bands at the time could have carried the deadweight of five dubious tracks but, whether by design or luck, the remaining tracks more than redressed the balance; on any other album they would have seemed good enough – here, they appeared superb. *Hello, I Love You* may have owed more than a little to the Kinks, but the performance was pure Doors, containing a classic Morrision image in "Sidewalk crouches at her feet/like a dog that begs for something sweet". More to the point, Jim was in good voice and sounding as if he were enjoying singing, as he did on *Love Street*, a rather lightweight piece until the final verse. The surviving portion of *Celebration Of The Lizard*, *Not To Touch the Earth*, was classic, menacing Doors, although the closing "I am the Lizard King/I can do anything" couplet would, given time, prove to be something of an albatross for Jim. Similarly menacing in the 'old' Doors tradition was *Unknown Soldier*, one of their best pieces of rock theatre but one which also transferred well onto vinyl. *Five To One* is at one and the same time an anti-establishment song, an indictment of the 'love generation', and an extremely subtle drug song. On whatever level it is taken, it works very well indeed.

The overall feel of a fragmented album was reinforced by the inclusion of the complete lyric to *Celebration Of The Lizard*, and the absence of a track called *Waiting For The Sun*

(both would appear on future albums). The (apparently) self-appointed Lizard King – a title the press were quick to pick up – explained his identification with the cold-blooded fraternity:

> *"The lizard and the snake are equated with the subconscious forces of evil... Even if you've never seen one, a snake seems to embody everything that we fear. It (Celebration Of The Lizard) is a kind of invitation to dark, evil forces,"*

a statement swiftly followed by a disclaimer, as if Jim realised that there was a fair chance that he would be misunderstood.

> *"It's all done tongue in cheek – I don't think people realise that it's not meant to be taken seriously. When you play the bad guy in a western, that's not you, that's just something you keep for the show. I don't really take it seriously... that's supposed to be ironic."*

The true irony lay in the fact that everyone else *did* take it seriously...

Immediately after the album was released, the Doors took to the road again, even though the disc required little, if any, pushing. The climax of the tour was to be a concert with the Who, at New York's Singer Bowl, a gig to be filmed for possible inclusion in the as-yet untitled documentary. Still pursuing his new policy of manipulating the crowd to relieve his boredom, Jim went through his entire gamut of theatrics, with the same effect as his Chicago performance had achieved some three months earlier. The fans fought with the police to rush the stage, heavy wooden chairs were thrown about and the concert was abandoned in the midst of the second Morrison-inspired riot. The Doors' underground reputation, which had suffered a severe knock with the release of *Waiting For The Sun*, regained some lost ground. Meanwhile, the band itself was gearing up for its first overseas tour in September and October, embracing the UK, Denmark, West Germany and Holland with co-headliners Jefferson Airplane.

At least, that's how the package was originally conceived and billed, but very
rapidly indeed, the Airplane were relegated

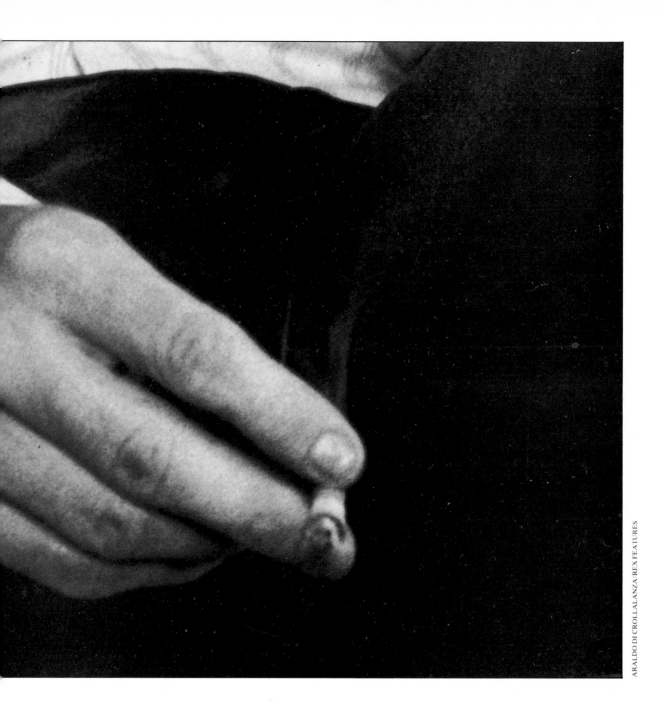

4

CHRIS WALTER/PHOTOFEATURES INT

to second slot and eventually all but ignored completely, as the Doors took the UK and Europe by storm. In the light of their reasonably dismal showings in the charts, with only *Hello, I Love You* having been anything like a hit, this may seem surprising, but there was a healthy underground/cult following in the UK for just about anything coming from the West Coast in 1967 and onwards (championed in the main by *Zig-Zag*), and the Doors were, quite simply, among the best of the bunch. Advance notices had even reached the ears of the British media, and the Granada TV company decided to use footage of the gigs at the Roundhouse, in London's Chalk Farm, for a documentary currently in production, concerning the not-inconsiderable social and political upheavals rocking the USA in 1968.

By playing the Roundhouse, the Doors were almost reliving their early Sunset Strip days; only comparatively recently vacated by British Rail, the Railway Roundhouse housed 2500 in conditions which could be described as 'intimate and uncomplicated'... or, alternatively, packed shoulder to shoulder with no seats and occasional falls of soot from the roof. For the Doors, it was an ideal setting, and the 10,000 tickets for their four shows sold out with startling rapidity. By the time the shows were over, the Doors' stature in the UK had attained legendary heights, remaining intact even when the TV film, *The Doors Are Open*, was broadcast in early October. Granada had chosen to film only the first concert and, whilst excellent by any standards, it wasn't as good as the other three. The film sound was so thin as to lose most of the power of the show and further diluting it was cross cut footage of the current unrest in America and the infamous 'Battle of Grosvenor Square' which had taken place outside the US Embassy earlier that year in London. Jim described the final show as "one of the best we've ever done", and further commented on *The Doors Are Open* thus:

> *"I thought the film was very exciting. To be on television, I think that's incredible. The thing is, the guys that made the film had a thesis of what it was going to be*

*before we even came over. We were going
to be the political rock group, and it also
gave them the chance to whip out some of
their anti-American sentiments, which they
thought we were going to portray, and so
they had their whole film before we came
over... but I still think they made an
exciting film."*

The remainder of the European tour was
equally well received and, surprisingly, contained only one instance of Jim publicly
over-indulging. This was in Amsterdam
when, after consuming more than even his
fair share of stimulants chased down with
booze, he interrupted the Airplane's set and,
after being 'helped' backstage, promptly
passed out and was rushed to the nearest
hospital, leaving Ray, Robbie and John to
perform as a trio. Reportedly, their collective
ill-humour was such that the performance
was exceptional...

It was whilst in London that Jim's poetic
aspirations received a boost, at the hands of
an American poet, Michael McClure.
McClure was impressed with Jim's poetry
and recommended private publication, therefore Jim's first call when he got back to Los
Angeles was to McClure's agent, to set the
wheels in motion.

Like *Celebration Of The Lizard* before
it, the film documentary was fast becoming
something of a white elephant. Some $30,000
had already been spent on the project, it was
nowhere near finished and only Jim thought
it worthwhile proceeding. Eventually, it was
decided to wrap the project up and do what
could be done with the existing material and,
with the Doors back in the studio rehearsing
songs for a new album, the editing was
handled by Frank Lisciandro, based on some
ideas from Jim.

The finished artefact was a curiously inconsequential affair. Entitled *Feast Of
Friends* (a line lifted from a poetic fragment
of Jim's which would later be incorporated in
a major composition, *An American Prayer*)
the movie showed the Doors on and off stage,
viewed with an air of near-lethargy, despite
the inclusion of the Singer Bowl footage of
the crowd storming the stage. An undoubted
reason for the overall feeling of detachment

was the curious decision to dispense with
'live' sound during most of the concert
sequences, in favour of the studio versions of
the same songs. As a result, *Feast Of Friends*
fell somewhere between Pennebaker's *Don't
Look Back* (a warts-and-all study of Bob
Dylan's 1965 UK tour) and the Beatles' *A
Hard Day's Night* with – to a non-Doors fan –
the redeeming features of neither. The concert scenes with 'live' sound were a vast
improvement on *The Doors Are Open* (snatches of which were utilised), but the backstage
scenes of the band, with Jim well to the fore,
relaxing, practising or improvising, failed to
generate enough lasting interest to maintain
the flow of the movie. As an historical
document, *Feast Of Friends* is invaluable, but
even despite the 'anything-that-is-art' ambi-
ence of the late sixties, it was a very ordinary
little film, its commercial potential extending
no further than that of a supporting short.

It was only after viewing the Singer Bowl
footage that Jim claimed to have suddenly
become aware of how he could manipulate
crowds.

*"The first time I saw that film, I was
pretty much taken aback, 'cause being
onstage, being one of the central figures, I
could only see it from my own viewpoint.
But then to see things as they really were...
I suddenly realised that I was, to a degree,
just a puppet, controlled by a lot of forces I
understood only vaguely."*

The dubious integrity of this statement was
borne out by the ensuing events as the Doors
embarked on their autumn tour; following
two peaceful opening dates, the concerts in
St. Louis, Cleveland, Phoenix and Chicago
were riddled with strife and riot. The event,
it seemed, had finally transcended the music;
for each person who came along to hear the
music, there seemed to be one who wanted to
see Jim drunk, stoned, sass a cop or incite a
riot – preferably all four – and was all too
ready and willing to respond to Jim's baiting.
Jim didn't deny anything, preferring to try
and explain it all as

"a joke, because it leads nowhere," or
*"just fun – we have fun, the cops have fun,
the kids have fun. It's a weird triangle..."*

Robbie viewed the escalating crowd prob-   **55**

lems, and their attendant police enforcement, with a more philosophical eye.

"It always bothered me to have police hanging around the concerts, waiting to bust us on any word or thing that we did... but we expected it. It was all part of the trip; there were two forces working, one force of change and the other force that wants things to stay the same and not be too far out, and there's always the balance that has to be present there at those situations."

The sessions for a new album began in December, during which time the band headlined a show at the Los Angeles Forum, on Friday the thirteenth. To the superstitious and rational alike, a Doors gig on such a date must have seemed an open invitation to disaster and, as the programme unfolded, the signs were ominous. Scant attention was paid to a Chinese folk musician; Jerry Lee Lewis played mostly country songs and was accordingly booed, whilst Sweetwater made the best of a bad job, shortened their set and got off as quickly as they could. The atmosphere was ripe for Jim to do something truly excessive, and this was apparently what the majority of the crowd had come to see.

"We can play music all night, if that's what you want,"

Jim told the crowd a little way into the set,

"but that's not what you want... you want something more, something different, something you ain't never seen before, don't you?... Well, fuck you, we came to play music!"

And they did, with Jim standing stock-still for most of the time, concentrating on singing. There was no riot, no encore... and, if anything, the critics felt more cheated than the fans. Wrote one commentator, "They (the fans) were bugged because they were cheated of their extra big moment – the moment when Morrison, they had read, would do something outrageous." If the fans had reason to be 'bugged' at anything, it was more likely to be the latest Doors single, *Touch Me*, a trailer from the album then in progress featuring a sound never before heard on a Doors record, that of a string ensemble. It also featured individual composer credits in place of the usual group credit

because Jim, concentrating more on his poetry than his music at the time, didn't want people to think that he'd written the musically acceptable but lyrically simple song. Accordingly, it was perhaps a little surprising when *Touch Me* quite rapidly rose up the charts, stopping at the number three position and remaining on the lists for thirteen weeks.

In January 1969, the Doors distanced themselves still further from the original fans by playing at Madison Square Garden and similar large venues, ostensibly to get the music across to greater numbers of the faithful, and gently ignoring the fact that the Doors' particular brand of music worked best in a relatively intimate atmosphere. There was also a feeling that the Doors, if not exactly *passé*, were becoming less and less relevant to the changing face of rock. The climate of rock music was also slowing down – in direct ratio, one suspects, to the increasing amount of assorted narcotics now becoming indispensable adjuncts to the business – as the emergence in 1969 of such bands as Chicago and Crosby, Stills & Nash testified. The Doors, too, were slowing down. They'd been together now for three years and were currently trapped between two camps – the critics who had begun to demand change (progression, it was called) and the fans, who by and large considered the band were doing a good job and wanted some more of the same, please (purists excepted, of course...). A further preview 45, *Wishful Sinful*, released in February, served to placate neither camp, as it contained not only more strings but also totally lacked any semblance of drive. It only reached forty-four – the Doors' worst chart placing to date – and it seemed for once the record-buying public was in accord with the critics.

February 1969 was *the* decisive month in the history of the Doors, though this observation is possible only with hindsight. Jim's increasing dissatisfaction with what his initial concept of the Doors and its music had become – mere entertainment – was reaching epic proportions and he began looking beyond music to restate his ideas, and to develop his creativity, which he feared was beginning to wane. In the fall of 1968, he'd read an article on the Living Theatre, which had stated,

> *"they are not really performers but a roving band of Paradise seekers, who define Paradise as total liberation, practising hypnology and advocating Paradise now. Their presence and function are in direct opposition to that repressive totalitarian state known as law and order,"*

a description which could accurately have been applied to the Doors in 1967. On hearing the troupe were to visit the University of Southern California in February 1969, he made reservations for all their performances and cornered some of the members, discussing techniques with them.

These techniques were not, in fact, too far removed from those Jim had been wont to use in the past, consisting of conducting a dialogue with the audience and obtaining a reaction by any means to hand, then using the results to comment on the prevalent political and moral strictures. Jim saw in the Living Theatre not only a vindication of his own original ideas but an extension of them and therefore a new avenue of creativity, one he decided to put into practice at a gig the next day, in Miami.

It seemed to be a dark-starred day from the very off-set. Jim missed both his flight in LA and his connection to Miami from New Orleans and arrived in Florida exceedingly drunk. The concert, which had already been delayed an hour, was therefore a shambles from the beginning with Jim making no more than a token attempt at singing, breaking off after a few lines to rap with – or rather *at* – the crowd as he had during the Living Theatre performance the day before, seeking response and becoming increasingly abusive when none was forthcoming. Finally, during *Touch Me*, Jim apparently decided desperate measures were required... and the legendary Miami Flash occurred – or did it?

> *"All I remember,"* says Robbie, *"was, it was a real hot night in Miami. We played at this place called the Dinner Key auditorium, which was used, I think, more for political speeches and stuff rather than rock shows. There was no air-conditioning or anything, so by the time we went on stage,*

POLICE DEPT
NEW HAVEN CONN
23750
12·10·67

*the place was a madhouse already – kids
were drunk, or on angel dust, or who
knows what... the place was crazed.
Before we went on stage, we were upstairs
in the dressing room and there were a
number of policemen up there, and we were
joking with them and everything, and
having a good time. We finally went down
and started to play, and Jim was in one of
his... more evil moods that night, I would
say. He'd just had a fight with his
girlfriend that day, and that didn't help
matters, and what happened was, there
was a lot of confusion onstage, and we
didn't play one of our best sets, I have to
admit. I remember starting one of the songs
about three times before we finally got into
it... but the kids were having a great time,
and the cops were having a great time –
they were laughing and boogie-ing around
– and then the allegation was that Jim had
whipped it out, in front of the audience,
right? Well, I personally never saw that
happen, nor did Ray or John, and out of
two or three hundred photographs that were
taken that night, there's not one shot that
shows that happening. There was a lot of
movement around on stage and jumping
around, and finally Jim jumped into the
audience and people were just milling
around – it looked like a scene from that
movie, The Snake Pit, where people are
just rushing around in endless waves. So
finally John and I – I don't know what
Ray did, but John and I scooted off the
stage because at that point about two or
three hundred people had jumped on the
stage and somebody yelled that the thing
was going to collapse, so we beat it
upstairs. I don't know how Jim got out of
there, but finally he managed to get back,
out of the audience and upstairs, and he
was pretty high by that point, I must
admit... and he had grabbed one of the
cop's hats and was fooling around, and
they were in a good mood and everything,
so finally we left, and we went off to
Jamaica for a little rest... and when we got
back, we found a warrant out for Jim's
arrest. We didn't know what it was for,
and nobody else did either. Finally we
learned what allegedly had happened, and
that was what the whole Miami trial was
about."*

Even allowing for an element of protective-
ness towards Jim on Robbie's part, it's
immediately obvious that, for someone who
was, at most, twenty feet or so away from Jim
at the time *not* to have seen anything does
rather argue against anything having taken
place. In their book, 'No One Here Gets Out
Alive', Jerry Hopkins & Danny Sugerman go
further and deny that anything *could* have
occurred as the Doors' road manager, Vince
Treanor, was standing behind Jim, holding
up his trousers and thus preventing any
possible flash.

Ray, somewhat perversely, contends that
something *did* occur, but remains infuriating-
ly vague as to its exact nature:

*"Jim said to the audience 'That's enough.
You didn't come here to hear music... you
didn't come here to see a good rock and roll
band – you came here for something you've
never seen before, something greater and
bigger than you've ever experienced...
What can I do? How 'bout if I show you
my cock? Isn't that what you want?' So he
took his shirt off and put it in front of
himself, and started dancing around, holding his shirt down, covering his groin, and
he pulled his shirt away – 'Did ya see it,
did ya see it, there it is, look, I did it, I did
it.'"*

However, this is getting somewhat ahead of
matters; after whatever is supposed to have
happened (or didn't...), the concert settled
into a shambolic groove, terminating when
Jim left the by-now crowded stage – either of
his own volition or thrown off by an over-
enthusiastic security guard – and the rest of
the band, fearing the stage was about to give
way, took this as the sign to wrap things up.

The following day, the Doors flew to the
Caribbean for a week's pre-arranged vacation, after which they would fly back to Los
Angeles to do further work on the new album
before embarking on a late spring touring
schedule. Back in Miami, however, the
moves which would ultimately lead to the
downfall of Jim Morrison and the Doors were
being instituted. Hysteria tinged the pro-

ceedings and the casual observer could be forgiven for thinking that a gross public outrage had occurred in Miami on March 1st, instead of an averagely chaotic rock concert; to the southern way of thinking, it would appear, the two were one and the same thing. It was almost as if there had never been a rock'n'roll show in Miami before, and while this is untrue, it is fair to say that there had never been anything like the Doors, and that the city powers were over-reacting to an unprecedented event.

And for a few days, that was all it was; blustering and cries of public indignation. It seemed the whole affair might blow over until the Wednesday following the concert, March 5th, when a complaint was lodged against Jim, charging him with indecent exposure, profanity, drunkenness and lewd and lascivious behaviour. The bust became front-page news within twenty-four hours. Jim had once said, not totally seriously,

> *"I think we're the band you love to hate – it's been that way from the beginning… We're universally despised, and I kinda relish the whole situation. Why, I don't know; I think that we're on a monstrous ego-trip, and people resent it… they hate us because we are so good!"*

The first the band knew about the furore was upon their return from Jamaica, and initially they treated it as a huge joke. Hearing there was going to be a 'Decency Rally' held in Miami, the Doors at once announced their own rally in California, which included flying the organiser of the Florida event to Los Angeles to receive a donation from the object of his abuse! Very soon, they discovered, there was precious little to laugh about, as the upcoming tour began falling apart at the seams; city after city cancelled and within days, the whole thing was abandoned. More worryingly, Doors' records were being denied airplay and suspended from radio playlists in major cities.

Needless to say, the press seized upon it and people who had previously never heard of the Doors, much less Jim Morrison, became instant experts on this latest 'wild man of rock' courtesy of their morning papers. When the FBI put out a warrant for

Jim's arrest at the end of March – on the dubious grounds of unlawful flight (viz. the Caribbean vacation) – any vestige of humour that remained vanished completely. Deciding the best course was to play along and hope everything would sort itself out, Jim turned himself in, was released with bail of $5000 and attempted to forget his worries by diving into a new film project, this time with his own HiWay Productions company (utilising the equipment and crew that had made *Feast Of Friends*) and into the private publication of *The Lords* and *The New Creatures*. Though *The Lords* is often described as poetry, it is actually largely a series of cinematic observations – often of stunning obscurity and banality – laced with a very few poems, and whatever merit it may have had in 1969 has largely evaporated, reading today as rather ordinary and undisciplined sixth-form/high school ramblings, accordingly pretentious and tedious by turns. *The New Creatures* was equally unrewarding to anyone not deeply into Jim and the Doors. Occasional lines and images sparkle and the poem beginning "The soft parade has now begun…" held together better than most, but in the main, it vacillated between almost Dadaist montage and that particular brand of sixties poetry which presumed anything vague and obscure enough to be deep and meaningful. But, perhaps the greatest failing of Jim's poetry was its inability to translate from performance to the printed page. Ray explains:

> *"Jim's poetry wasn't necessarily written poetry. I always considered him to be back in the classic Greek tradition of a spoken poet, a man who gets up on the stage and recites his poetry to handclaps or a drum beat, or to an implied beat. Jim always had that implied sense of rhythm in his poetry."*

Whilst Jim was immersing himself in his films and verse, the rest of the band were plugging away at the new album sessions, cutting tracks for Jim to dub his vocals over when he felt like doing so. In May, the third preview 45, *Tell All The People* was released, and, so prominent was the brass section, one could have been forgiven for thinking it was a Chicago single and not one by the Doors. **61**

Musically, it wasn't that bad, but the arrangement coupled with the media blackout on Doors products (as opposed to Doors news...) ensured that the disc got no further than number fifty-seven. Doors afficianados with half an eye open would by now have noted that the last three A sides were Krieger compositions, and could well have wondered what Jim was doing to occupy his time if not recording.

In June, *The Soft Parade* was released to general critical disdain; if *Waiting For The Sun* had been somewhat indecisive, this latest offering was positively confused. The tracks are sharply divided between those with string and/or brass arrangements and those without, and not so sharply split betweeen filler and worthwhile material. The latter is comprised, in the main, of the tracks Jim contributed – with the glaring exception of *Do It*, a strong contender for the worst Doors' song ever. The remainder of the first side ranges from the indifferent to the almost acceptable. *Touch Me* and *Tell All The People* suffer from superfluous horn/string arrangements, dubious lyrics and an apparent lack of commitment from Jim. *Easy Ride* at least seems to capture his interest, but not even a typically Morrisonesque final verse can make up for a decidedly shaky country and western track. Only *Shaman's Blues* approaches the 'old' Doors standards in feel and execution. *Wild Child* opens the second side with the promise of better things to come, despite two utterly disposable spoken lines. The opening to *Running Blue* similarly promises much but this hope is rapidly dashed by those seemingly ubiquitous horns and an utterly incongruous middle eight in the best (?) hillbilly tradition. *Wishful Sinful* is easily the blandest Doors track to date, being nothing more nor less than cocktail lounge listening; neither good nor bad, just irrelevant.

What rescues *The Soft Parade* from near terminal mediocrity is the title track, one of Morrison's best works, musically and lyrically, and one which has improved with time. Considering the highly diverse elements comprising the song, it works exceedingly well, although Jim's opening oration hasn't aged as gracefully as the rest of the piece and is now truly cringeworthy. Luckily, everything that follows is truly excellent in a convoluted sort of way, with everyone performing as well as they ever did. Jim's valedictory pronouncement,

> "*When all else fails, we can whip the horses' eyes / and make them sleep / and cry*"

is either as pompous as his opening rap, or depending on how it's taken, the key to most of his lyrics, translating roughly as,

> "when inspiration fails, slip in a couple of non sequiturs and nonsense lines, and it'll all look rather impressive, 'cause no-one is going to admit they don't know what the hell it all means."

It could be argued that *The Soft Parade* sounds the way it does due to the circumstances under which it was recorded... but as two singles had been issued before the Miami happening, this hypothesis doesn't really stand up to examination. The facts are that Jim was devoting more energy to his poetry and film projects, and that the Doors as a whole were coasting a little on their success, becoming a little self-indulgent musically whilst at the same time running a little low on ideas. John:

> "*Just to show how ridiculous things got on that album, we imported Jesse McReynolds and Jimmy Buchanan, a fiddler and a picker, from North Carolina to play one solo on one song,* Running Blue. *We had a great time making that album... we spent probably more than $80,000 on that one – we were making our* Sgt. Pepper."

With such a costly album to cover, not to mention steadily rising legal costs, the Doors desperately needed concert income and finally, some three months after Miami, some dates were confirmed – with strings attached, the strings being a $5,000 a show deposit, redeemable only if the show passed the moral scrutiny of the promoters, the city fathers and other, self-appointed, arbiters of public decency. These strictures had the unexpectedly good effect of causing the shows to be tighter and more musically impressive than they had been for a very long time. As the summer wore on, Doors' shows became more frequent – though hardly plentiful – and the ever-present threat of further legal harassment if Jim stepped out of line again continued. At one show, the band were greeted backstage by the local sheriff waving warrants for the arrest of each member of the band, to be signed – or not – depending on how he thought they performed that night.

A welcome escape at the end of July were concerts in Mexico City, providing a respite from the increasingly oppressive American scene. The shows, and the audience response, were well up to the new standard. Back in the USA, however, it was business as before, with shows still very hard to set up, and promoters still cancelling. The only concerts at which the Doors appeared in the whole of July were at the end of the month in the Aquarius Theatre, Los Angeles. These were the band's first hometown shows for some months and were being recorded for possible inclusion on the live album for which Elektra was now pressing to help offset the cost of *The Soft Parade*. (Whilst seldom popular with the bands themselves, live albums are guaranteed sellers.) A degree of media backlash still prevailed; according to the LA Times, Jim's singing was "quite timid, his range ever-decreasing", Ray's

UPI

63

organ was "his usual pedestrian effort", whilst John's drumming "made up for in enthusiasm what it lacked in technique." Only Robbie, "as tasteful and imaginative as usual", emerged with any credit, it appeared. A swift survey of almost any other review of the shows leads to the conclusion that the Times writer either had something against the Doors or didn't actually bother to go along to the theatre because, without exception, every other report of the concerts was an unabashed rave, many welcoming the Doors back "fully cleansed after the unfortunate after-effects of their highly-publicised Miami exhibition." July generally marked the re-acceptance of the band by the media with several lengthy articles appearing. In the forefront of these was Jim's *Rolling Stone* interview with Jerry Hopkins, which is possibly one of the most articulate interviews ever given by a rock personality, ranging through the history of the Doors to religion and morality and winding up with Jim's explanation of his now-legendary alcoholic intake;

> "*You're in complete control, up to a point.It's your choice, every time you take a sip... I guess it's the difference between suicide and slow capitulation.*"

The printed interview closed with a new, long poem of Jim's, as yet untitled and vastly superior to anything to be found in *The New Creatures*. What gave Jim possibly the greatest pleasure was the author's credit at the foot of the page: James Douglas Morrison (poet).

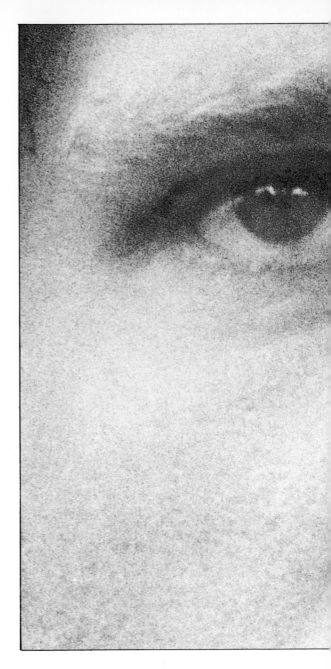

Throughout the remainder of the summer of 1969, Jim occupied himself with discussing future cinematic projects (all of which, for one reason or another, failed to go beyond the talking stage), finishing off the movie project begun in the spring, now named *HWY*, and writing material for a new studio album. Once again, the strictures of the previous months had combined to boost the creativity he had feared was beginning to flag; perhaps his recent abortive film projects had persuaded him that music was, after all, the best vehicle by which to express his views and feelings.

Legal problems, and the Miami affair, still made life exceedingly wearing, however. In early November, Jim returned to the scene of the 'crime' to enter a "Not Guilty" plea and was again released on bail of $5000, the trial itself being set for the following year, in April. Within days, Jim was once again in trouble, this time as a result of an impulse decision to go and see a Rolling Stones concert. He, and those with him, never actually got to see the show, for as soon as the plane touched down in Phoenix, they were

arrested, and it must be admitted that their

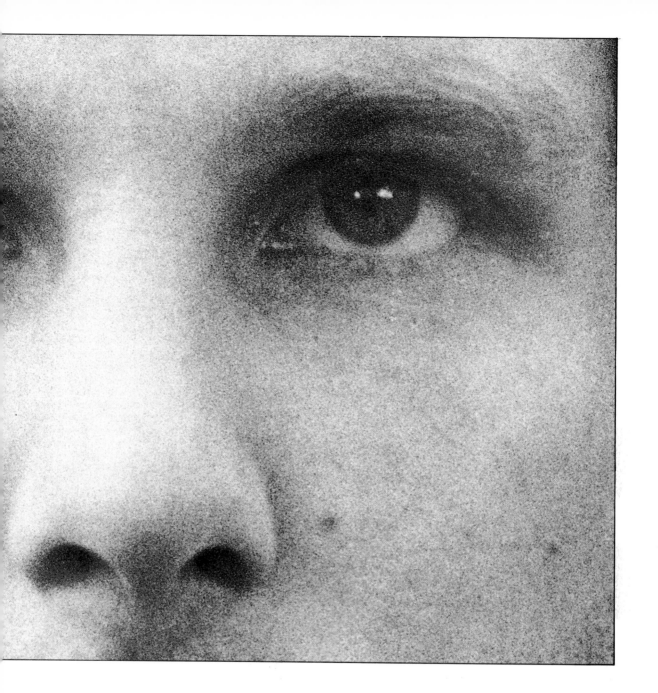

5

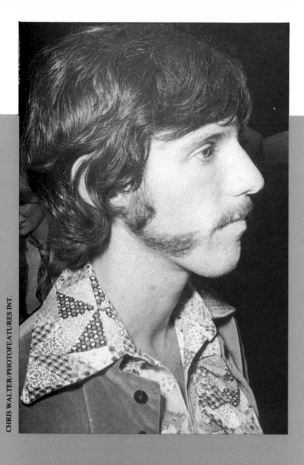

in-flight behaviour was reportedly something short of impeccable. Normally, such an escapade would have counted for very little, but not only was there the cloud of Miami still hanging over Jim, but, due to a recent spate of hijackings, a new law had been passed relating to interfering with the flight of an aircraft (a vague and woolly phrase, designed to cover almost every eventuality), one which could result in a ten-year prison sentence plus a hefty fine... and it was under this law that Jim was charged, in addition to the almost-customary drunk and disorderly.

Fortunately, Jim had little time to brood on this latest turn of events for the Doors were recording their next album and, for once, it was relatively easy going. The horns and strings were dispensed with because, according to Robbie,

> *"We listened to* The Soft Parade *a couple of times and decided that it would probably sound just as good without the brass."*

It wasn't all plain sailing, however, as Jim often took several hours to complete one vocal take. Both *Feast Of Friends* and *HWY* had received bad reviews, although *Feast* had been awarded a Gold Medal at the Atlanta International Film Festival, and the other Doors considered any film projects with suspicion, as they tended to divert Jim's energies away from music.

As the new decade of the seventies dawned, the Doors were still finding it hard to set up concerts, which threatened the live album project, but eventually two shows towards the end of January were set for New York, at the Felt Forum. The concerts were good, proving to the largely New York based rock critics and papers that, despite everything, the Doors were still capable of producing the goods on stage.

The release of *Morrison Hotel* the following month demonstrated that they could similarly still cut it on disc for, despite a rather weak ending – *Indian Summer* and *Maggie M'Gill* being somewhat inconsequential – the album emerged as the Doors' strongest offering since *Strange Days*. *Roadhouse Blues*, the one-time title track, allowed Robbie to trade some burning licks with one Giovanni Puglese on harmonica (John Sebastian using

71

what is claimed to be his real name), but
unfortunately also emphasised the fact that
Jim's voice wasn't quite what it once had
been, sounding decidedly rough around the
edges, a point underscored by the following
track. *Waiting For The Sun* gave every sign of
being a 1968 track with some 1969/70 overdubs, in particular Ray's Moog; generally, it
might have been suitable for the earlier
album, swinging between heavy power and
light touches of Doors menace with good
vocals from Jim. *You Make Me Real* is really
little more than head-down straightforward
rock, but that the Doors were doing it, and
with nary a string in earshot, was cause for
celebration. *Peace Frog* bears all the hallmarks of classic Doors, even Jim's spoken
lines dovetailing neatly into the general
scheme, which at one and the same time
surveyed America as the Sixties drew to a
close and allowed Jim to loose some pent-up
feeling – "Blood in the streets of the town of
New Haven" must have been a very sweet
line to sing. The coda, *Blue Sunday*, unlike
some of Jim's other more obvious material, is
oddly effective. The allegory contained in
Ship Of Fools is a little forced, but the music
more than compensates for any lyrical shortcomings. Pursuing the nautical theme, *Land
Ho!* opens with a finely-drawn character
sketch before switching to an apparently
completely different subject altogether,
though it could be argued that the latter
verses offer a different view of the same
person, a glimpse at the darker side everyone
possesses... *The Spy* shares with the early
Doors canon a moody atmosphere, but there
all similarity ends. *Queen Of The Highway*
sounds innocuous enough at first but with
repeated hearings, an autobiographical element manifests itself, evolving into a hope for
the future, a concept about which Jim had
never previously been that concerned.

As noted before, the album closes with two
fairly tame cuts, but the overall feeling of a
band once considered as having lost its
direction and drive returning at little short of
full power on the tracks and, to a degree,
back to the basics, shines through, and the
reviews in general reflected this, *Rolling
Stone* supplying the only dissenting voice.

The record-buying public, who, after all, have the final say in these matters, chose to side with the majority view, propelling *Morrison Hotel* to number four and holding it in the lists for over six months, a noteworthy feat considering that it was the first ever Doors' album not to be trailered with a single.

Another interesting aspect of this fifth LP was the confusion over the title; in some circles, it's known as *Morrison Hotel/Hard Rock Cafe*, these being the titles of the two sides. It's a more than reasonable possibility that, had the front and back sleeve shots been reversed, the album would now be known as *Hard Rock Cafe*, as it seems Elektra assumed whatever appeared on the front slick had to be the title!

The following month, a double A side single, *You Make Me Real/Roadhouse Blues*, was pulled from the LP and just scraped into the top 50, a somewhat better performance than the previous release, *Running Blue*, which struggled to make it to sixty-four.

Not that this was of much concern to Jim at the time, for it was towards the end of March that he returned to Phoenix to answer the charges relating to his November 1969 arrest. During the farcical trial in which a stewardess, the chief prosecution witness, continually confused Jim's actions with those of another member of his party that day, he was found guilty of assault, whilst the more serious federal charge was dropped. At the sentencing a fortnight later, that same witness had decided to change her testimony, and the sentencing was deferred for a further fortnight.

A small lightening of the gloom surrounding Jim (and therefore the Doors) came in early April with the publication by Simon & Schuster of *The Lords & The New Creatures*, in one hardback volume. But it was just a small sparkle; the black cloud of Miami still hung ominously over every gig and, as the recording of the live album was still in progress, the pressures were doubled. Inevitably, something had to give and it happened in Boston; the show was running late and the hall owners decided to throw the switches and cut the power. Unluckily for Jim, his

74 microphone was somehow still live, and his

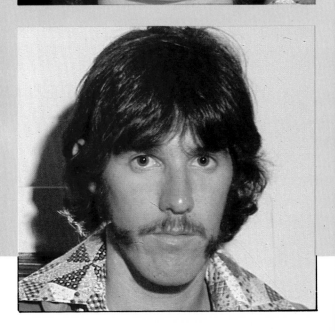

less-than-charitable views about the plug being pulled echoed throughout the hall. The following morning, the band learned a show scheduled for that day was cancelled.

One possible stress factor *was* removed, however, when Jim returned to Phoenix for a final time and had all charges against him dismissed, the stewardess having finally sorted out who was who and reversed her evidence. On the other hand, the Miami trial, originally scheduled for April, had been repeatedly put back, and was now set to take place in August. Whilst this gave Jim's attorneys more time to prepare a defence, it also afforded Jim more time to brood on the subject, and he began talking openly of getting away from it all once the trial was over, and going to Paris, an artistic centre which had long held his interest.

In the event, Jim made it to France before the Miami trial came to pass, after concluding a verbal deal with MGM to appear in, and co-produce, two films. En route to Europe, Jim stopped off in New York to deliver the live album tapes to Elektra for editing and mastering prior to release, and also to take part in one of the more bizarre episodes of his life. Staying with Patricia Kennely, the editor of *Jazz & Pop*, a magazine generally favourable to the Doors down the years, he suddenly decided to marry her. Nor was it to be an ordinary ceremony, but a Wicca, or witches, wedding (and therefore of dubious legality, and most likely not recognised as a binding contract) as Patricia was a practising member of a New York coven. The following Saturday, Jim left with a friend for Paris where for a week he did the usual tourist trip, seeing the sights, interspersed with the usual Morrison drinking bouts, before moving on to Spain and North Africa for a further two weeks. He got back to Los Angeles just in time to see *Absolutely Live* released and suffer a recurrence of the pneumonia he had contracted whilst in New York.

> *"I think it's a true document of one of our good concerts. It's not insanely good, but it's a true portrait of what we usually do on a good night"*

was Jim's opinion of *Absolutely Live* and, glossing over the fact that rather than being a

single show, the album is comprised of songs from at least three different concerts separated quite widely by time and distance (the shows being in LA, New York and Philadelphia), this is a very fair summary. As is the case with most live albums recorded before the days of 'sweetening' and post-dubbing, there are quite a few vocal and musical fluffs, and some of the performances are rather lackadaisical. Balanced against these points is the inclusion of more new material than is customarily to be found on such albums. The choice of a promoter's crowd admonitions for the album's opening 'track' seems unique and not far short of inspired! *Who Do You Love* is standard Doors' treatment of an oldie, notable only for its being overlong, some screaming guitar from Robbie and for Ray being slightly, but most definitely, out of tune. The ensuing medley is successful only in reducing all of the songs within to a repetitive plod, and is a strong argument for any similar arrangement being banned by law! *Love Hides*, in fact, shows every sign of being an on-the-spot (at the most, semi-rehearsed) improvisation. *Build Me A Woman*, another new title, never really gets much further than a 12-bar sexual strut whilst *When The Music's Over*, shorn of its studio immediacy, is further despoiled by Jim's censure of the crowd – for once his control seemed to have slipped and he was reduced to pleas ("Now is that any way to behave at a rock'n'roll concert?") and finally threats; "You don't wanna hear that for the next half hour, do you?" referring to Ray's two-note organ riff.

The third side opens with a rather amusing rap from Jim, promising "something special... no, not that!" before venturing into the realms of security and back to Miami. The 'something special' turns out to be a decidedly limp performance by Ray of an equally limp new John Lee Hooker cover, *Close To You*. Luckily *Universal Mind* makes good any lapse in quality or pace by being a good, menacing song in the 'old' Doors mould. *Break On Through 2* is apparently so named in deference to Jim's newly improvised opening and reworking of other parts of the tune, sad to say not a patch on mark 1.

The fourth side of the album, however, more than compensated for any preceding shortcomings, as the now legendary *Celebration Of The Lizard* finally became public domain, and proved itself to be one of Jim's most impressive works, tying together in a single reasonably coherent package all his dominant themes and ideas. The sections are musically very diverse (one of the reasons the studio version had to be abandoned), but somehow the fragmented quality of a live performance serves to unite and the result is both effective and affecting. This 'captured' version includes a few verses not printed on the *Waiting For The Sun* sleeve and, more interestingly, omits the couplet for which Jim was ultimately remembered – "I am the Lizard King, I can do anything". The song-poem closes rather anti-climatically with Jim intoning in a very matter-of-fact voice, but in fact, in the light of the preceding twenty or so minutes, there's no other way it could close. The album itself ends with *Soul Kitchen* performed in a suitably rousing manner. As expected, sales were brisk and the double set reached number eight in the charts, ironically entering the lists the day after Jim flew to Miami for his long-delayed obscenity trial.

Jim was represented by Max Fink, as he had been during the Phoenix episode, and Fink had prepared a lengthy brief intended to outline how Jim's behaviour that night was perfectly in keeping with the tenor of the times. Taken overall, it was an impressive document and, reading through, Jim began to believe that he had, at least, a fighting chance, a feeling reinforced by Max's handling of the Phoenix affair. "You know, I'm beginning to believe I might be innocent," he remarked to the other Doors the morning of the trial, a rather brave statement in view of the fact – which Jim almost certainly knew – that the presiding judge would be up for re-election in November and that his conviction of an anti-establishment figure would hardly harm the judge's prospects.

Proceedings that first day were, to say the least, brief. Judge Goodman had decided that his schedule that day was too taxing and put the trial back a further two days. Thus it wasn't until Wednesday, August 12th that the trial proper commenced, with the swearing-in of the jury another two days later on Friday. Jim's new-found confidence must have taken a severe knock. The Los Angeles Free Press observed

> "Jurors in Florida, although half in number, are apparently twice as good as elsewhere. They are also twice as old; the youngest juror is forty-two, the rationale apparently being that anyone under the age of thirty is necessarily prejudiced..."

Jim's counsel, not surprisingly, objected to the jury on the grounds that they could hardly be counted as among Jim's peers. The judge noted this and adjourned for the weekend.

On the following Monday, and with the jury unchanged, the trial proper began with the formal reading of the charges, the defence's opening address and the first of the witnesses for the prosecution taking the stand. By the end of the day, Jim's hopes had taken an upward swing as Max had methodically cross-examined the witnesses and showed up the glaring inconsistencies between their statements taken shortly after the incident and their testimony on the stand. This encouraging trend continued until the sixth witness for the prosecution was called; the chances of this gentleman tripping himself up were minimal, for it was he who had filed the original complaint. Not even the persuasive talents of Max Fink could find fault with Robert Jennings' conviction that Jim had exposed himself "for between five and eight seconds". However, during his spell on the witness stand, an interesting and possibly significant fact came to light – that Jenkins and other members of his family were in the employ of the state attorney. This prompted one LA paper to comment

> "Miami justice being what it is, we might all soon have friend and Doors singer Jim Morrison literally in the house of detention... his trial seems to be another establishment attempt to subvert an emerging new culture; what the establishment cannot usurp, it must suppress and repress."

The following day, Thursday, August 20th, would normally have been a 'rest' day, but as

the Doors were contracted to perform in California on the Friday and Saturday, Judge Goodman agreed to carry over and then adjourn until the following Tuesday. The single witness remembered seeing nothing untoward and was backed up by some 150 photographs taken that night, all reasonably innocuous. Then, out of the blue, the judge handed down a shattering ruling; no evidence concerning 'community standards' would be deemed permissible. This effectively undermined Fink's defence and he argued against the ruling, in vain. Judge Goodman, for whatever reasons, was intractable... and suddenly Jim's future looked bleak.

The Doors completed the California shows and were back in Miami on the Tuesday, to witness the convincing prosecution evidence of four police officers, all of whom averred they had either seen or heard an obscene word or gesture. The next day, Jim allowed an audience tape of the show to be played to the jury, hardly the wisest of moves bearing in mind the age, politics and geographic origins of the jurors, and it may well have sealed his fate.

Another victim of the Miami trial was the Doors' second tour of Europe; however, one engagement was fulfilled, at the second Isle of Wight festival. The Doors had never really liked the idea of performing in the open air, but now it was a matter of finance rather than personal preference which dictated the situation. So Saturday 29th August found them on a stage, performing before a crowd of some half a million and performing rather badly as Jim readily admitted when cornered by one of the authors of this book backstage the following day.

"I didn't have such a good time last night, because I had to perform, and I'd only just gotten off the plane." He added: *"I can see why people like it... I think all these people who say that huge festivals are over and dead, all that, I think they're wrong – I think the festival is going to become increasingly significant in the next three, four, five years. At the same time, I'm sure these things get highly romanticised. When I saw the Woodstock film, it seemed just like a bunch of young parasites being*

spoonfed this three or four days of... well, you know. They looked like dupes, victims of a culture more than an emerging one... but that might have been sour grapes, because I wasn't there, not even as a spectator. So I think that, even though they can be a mess and might not be what they pretend to be, it's still better than nothing, and I'm sure some of the people take away a kind of myth back to the city with them, and it'll affect them."

From here it seemed a natural progression to the politics of revolution, but Jim with Miami forever at the back of everthing, was slightly reticent;

"I don't want to say too much because I haven't studied politics that much really. It just seems that you have to be in a constant state of revolution, or you're dead. It has to be a constant thing, not something that's going to change things and that's it... it has to be every day."

Before disappearing for some well-earned rest, Jim hinted at further literary ideas and aspirations –

"I'd like to start a magazine, a newspaper thing in LA, but I'd only do it if I could finance it myself, so I wouldn't have to advertise... one of those little magazines, a manifesto like the Surrealists and Dadaists used to put out"

– and considering what was happening to him, made an amazing comment on his trial:

"It's actually a very fascinating thing to go through... a thing you can observe."

For all his seeming nonchalance, Jim was still very concerned about what might be awaiting him back in America and was also disenchanted with performing live to the extent of deciding that, indifferent as it was, the Isle of Wight was to be his last live appearance.

On Wednesday, September 2nd, the prosecution rested its case, and before calling witnesses of its own, Jim's defence entered a plea for acquittal arguing that as the State's case had been shown to be inherently contradictory, reasonable doubt had been raised. It was at best a half-hearted gesture, and no-one was unduly surprised when it was passed over. The prepared defence having been ruled out of order, Max Fink could do little

but parade witnesses who would counter the prosecution's claims. They sounded most convincing, as had the witnesses for the prosecution, and an air of stalemate began to pervade the proceedings. After a lengthy recess and some dozen more defence witnesses – including the Doors themselves – the trial ended and the jury withdrew. After two and a half hours it returned, acquitting Jim of lewd behaviour and drunkenness whilst convicting him of profanity. On the subject of indecent exposure, it was undecided... until the following day, when Jim was found guilty on that charge as well. Bail was set at $50,000 and sentencing was to take place in October. If he were honest with himself, Jim must have known that there was never any doubt as to the outcome, merely the degree of it; nonetheless, he was stunned.

The news of Jimi Hendrix's death – on the day Jim was sentenced – hardly helped his depression (Jim had appeared with Jimi on *Blues Blues*, a studio jam recorded earlier in 1970 which contained the prophetic line, "Woke up this morning/found myself dead", a title by which it was also known), which was increased a few weeks later when another friend, Janis Joplin, also died.

In sombre mood, Jim returned to Miami at the end of October to be sentenced. As expected the maximum penalty was levied; a $500 fine and six months hard labour in a Florida jail. Max Fink swiftly filed an appeal.

The trial had had a detrimental effect on the Doors' relationship with Elektra, and the release of *13*, the Doors' first compilation album, strained it still further. The company wanted product, both for the traditionally lucrative Christmas market and to make up for the relatively poor sales of *Absolutely Live* (despite its respectable chart showing).

"We never wanted them to do that – we had nothing to do with those albums at all,"

says Ray. Nonetheless, as compilations go, *13* – the number of tracks – was better selected and programmed than most and, running a shade under three-quarters of an hour, was exceedingly good value. It didn't, in fact, sell that well, reaching only number twenty-five, far and away the worst Doors album chart placing.

Almost as if in protest, the Doors began rehearsing songs for a new album, their last required by the Elektra contract. It came together quite rapidly as quite a lot of the material was already written and in the case of one number had been in the band's live act since 1966. Having rehearsed the songs, the band called in Paul Rothchild, who listened to the material and astounded everyone by announcing he didn't want to produce the album, as he considered the material, performance and general attitude well below par.

> *"The band had been in rehearsal, trying to get a new album together. I went to several of them, and Jim especially was really bored... couldn't really get himself up for it. I said, 'This album is going to be a disaster.' One moment, I just got up, went into the studio and said, 'Hey listen – I'm bored. First time in my life when I've been in the studio that I've had my head down on the console. I love you guys, and I love the music, but it seems to me that you're doing nothing to me and I'm doing nothing to you. I want both our careers to survive, so why don't you go on and produce yourselves?'"*

Robbie remembers things slightly differently;

> *"It was a mutual thing, actually. We found that after four or five albums, a group learns how to get what they want in the studio, and Paul didn't really have anything to say that we didn't think of already ourselves, so he wasn't a necessary factor anymore. He didn't feel that he was contributing enough to really be the producer. He was one of those producers who really has to get his whole trip into the thing and put his whole energy into the thing, into what he's doing, and we knew at this time what we wanted..."*

The Doors decided to co-produce the album with engineer Bruce Botnick and, more importantly, to record it in the rehearsal room below the Doors office. Ray takes up the story;

> *"It was back to basics, back to the roots. We brought microphones and recording equipment right into the rehearsal studio... Instead of going into a professional studio, we said, 'Hey, let's record this album where we rehearse, and let's have a spontaneous, live kind of feel.' We brought in Jerry Scheff on bass and Marc Benno on rhythm guitar – we had never used a rhythm guitar player before – so we had six musicians all going at the same time. The song LA Woman is a live take – Jim sang the song while we played it. There's a minimum of overdubs; I think I overdubbed a tack piano on LA Woman, and that's about it, everything else was an actual live recording, as if it was done on stage. That's why it sounds so fresh."*

Jim was similarly enthusiastic;

> *"At last, I'm doing a blues album."*

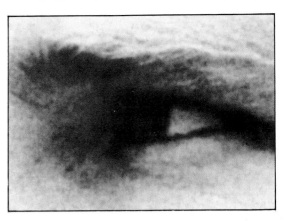

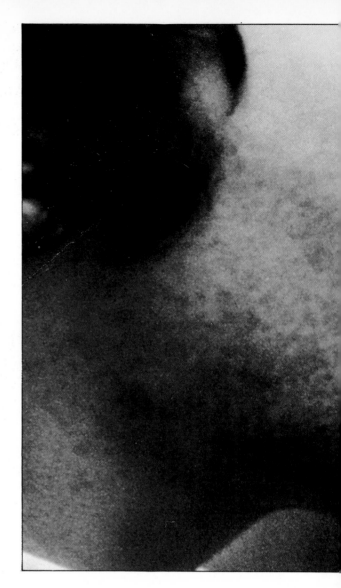

As enthusiastic as he professed to be concerning the new album, Jim hadn't laid up all his previous interests for the sake of music and, with his vocal chores completed fairly rapidly, once more turned his attention to cinematic ideas... but, as ever, the project failed to progress beyond the talking (and drinking) stage.

A spur-of-the-moment notion which not only came to pass but also, with the passing of time, achieved legendary status, was the poetry recording session conducted on Jim's birthday, December 8th 1970. Whatever the impulse that caused him to celebrate this twenty-seventh birthday engaged in creative endeavour rather than alcoholic debauch, it was a fortunate one, for it allowed Jim's verse to be appreciated in its correct context, that of live performance as opposed to dry printed text. The poems he recited at the Village Recorders that night were, with the exception of *An American Prayer*, previously un-published. As the session progressed Jim took to using a tambourine to establish a rhythm or highlight a word or phrase, and involved sundry spectators. Frank Liscian-
84 dro underscored the reason why Morrison

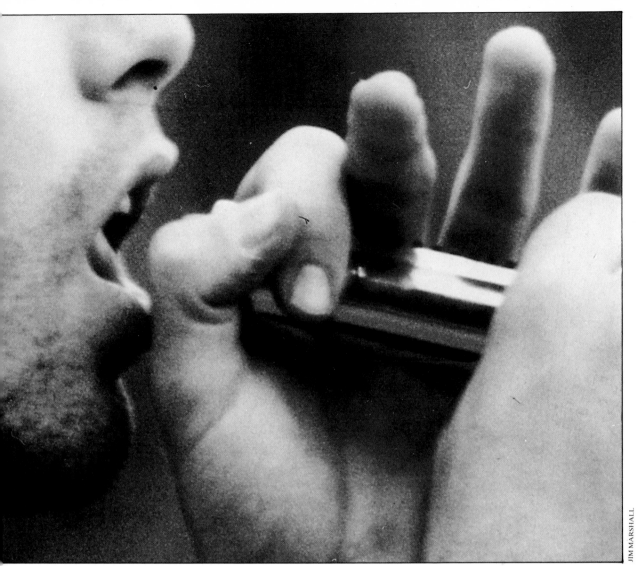

6

UPI

verse spoken and printed are such disparate entities when he observed,

"He was using words not so much for their logic as for their emotive effect... the words didn't have to mean *so much as imply or suggest. He used words to create a vast mural of feeling; I felt like a swimmer in a heavy sea – it was alright as long as I let the swell of words carry me along, but if I tried to fathom the meaning or understanding, I was quickly underwater."*

Despite becoming drunk towards the end of the session, the experience of actually getting what he considered to be his real work down on tape raised Jim's spirits enough for him to agree to reverse his 'no more live shows' policy, and concerts in Dallas and New Orleans were hurriedly set up.

That the public still wanted to see the band was evident by the speed at which twelve thousand seats – six thousand per show – were snapped up in Dallas. A sneak preview of *Riders On The Storm* went down sufficiently well for the band, and especially Jim, to feel that they had found their way again. The feeling, however, lasted less than twenty-four hours, for in New Orleans the following night, December 12th 1970, the music *was* finally over. Why is something of a mystery; perhaps Jim had expended all his reserves in Dallas. As Ray noted,

"Anyone who was there that night saw it. Jim just... lost all his energy halfway into the set. You could almost see it leave him; he hung on to the mike stand and his spirit just slipped away. He was finally drained, I guess."

Over the 1970/71 winter period, whilst the Doors put the finishing touches to the new album tracks, Jim was once more involving himself in other things. A poetry album with Elektra was being discussed and there were talks with Simon & Schuster concerning a paperback edition of *The Lords & The New Creatures*. Similarly, if on a less formal level, Jim was considering film and theatrical projects with his old friends from U.C.L.A. days Larry Marcus and Fred Myrow, a somewhat strange move considering he was planning to leave America for a while. Having consummated his affair with Los

Angeles on this new album, he'd decided to take a break and return to Paris for an extended sabbatical. Ray:

"Jim left for Paris right in the middle of the mixing of L.A. Woman *– I think we had maybe two more songs to mix – and he said, 'Hey man, everything's going fine here. Why don't you guys finish it up? Pam and I are going to Paris, and we're just gonna hang out for a while, see what happens.' So we said, 'OK, talk to you later. Go over there and have a good time, relax, take it easy. Write some poetry.' What Jim wanted to do in leaving for Paris was to immerse himself in an artistic environment, to get away from Los Angeles, to get away from rock 'n' roll, to get away from all the sensational press that he had. Jim was hounded by a lot of sensational press; a lot of yellow journalism associated with the man and, frankly, he was tired of it. He was tired of being 'The Lizard King'. Jim Morrison was a poet. He was an artist, he didn't want to be the king of orgasmic rock, the king of acid rock, the Lizard King. He felt all those titles that people had put on him were demeaning to what the Doors were trying to do, so in an effort to escape that, and to re-charge his artistic batteries, he went to Paris, the city of art. He was going to write, maybe look into a few film projects – Agnes Varda had contacted him about doing a movie, as had Jacques Demis and also, back in the States, Steve McQueen had talked to him about doing some films. So Jim was just getting away, taking a breather, a rest... going to become a poet again. And we had finished our commitment to Elektra; we had to deliver seven records over that five or six year period of time. So we had completed our contract, and were free to go to a new record company, continuing making records,* not *make records, whatever. So, we decided to just take a long hiatus, and there was really no reason for Jim to be there for the mix. He said, 'You guys finish it up, I'm going to Paris.' We said, 'OK man, see you later...and I haven't heard from him since."*

In the same month as Jim joined Pamela in Paris, the Doors' first single for a year was released. *Love Her Madly* b/w *(You Need Meat) Don't Go No Further* proved to be one of the Doors' best selling singles and, despite the uninspired blues B-side sung by Ray, it reached number eleven in the charts.

The following month, April, saw the release of not only the Doors' first original studio album in over a year but also the reissue of four of their top thirty hit tracks in the form of two back-to-back singles, *Light My Fire/Love Me Two Times* and *Touch Me/Hello, I Love You*. Elektra, it appeared, was none too confident of the Doors renewing their contract and were endeavouring to get as much mileage as they could out of existing material. However, neither single made the charts.

By comparison – by contrast – the other April 1971 Doors release, *L.A. Woman* sold in substantial quantities and, more importantly, received full critical approbation. *Rolling Stone*, the most influential mag of the time and one which had previously had a considerable down on the Doors, announced that the album was

"The Doors' greatest album (including their first) and the best album so far this year..."

Jim's assertion that he was finally making a blues record was correct, for this was the most blues-oriented Doors album to date, something of a surprise considering the wide time span of the material. Also surprising is the fact that the worst performed song was *Crawling King Snake*, an old John Lee Hooker standard and a staple of the Doors early stage repertoire. Possibly it was resurrected in order to fill a gap on the album (if so, it was hardly necessary, for even without the song, *L.A. Woman* clocks in at just under three-quarters of an hour); but in any case, it was a bad choice as the performance of the piece is utterly lifeless. Fortunately, the remainder of the performances had evidently captured the band's, and especially Jim's interest, and the notion of recording the majority of the track for each song 'live', leaving only a few vocal and instrumental sections to be later overdubbed, had paid dividends. *The Changeling*, dating lyrically, if not musically, from 1968, opened the album with a commanding walking-bass figure whilst the organ and guitar initially competed, then complemented each other over the same phrase. The instrumentation was basic Doors, Robbie supplying incisive fuzz guitar towards the close. In the manner of *Back Door Man*, Jim opened with assorted grunts and groans... but when he weighed in with the actual lyric, it was at once obvious that the bottle had finally taken its toll and by the end of the song, Jim was having to work hard to keep it from cracking completely, despite the song being very much on one level throughout. This could, of course, be one reason for a return to the 'live' one-take days; on the evidence of *L.A. Woman*, it seems doubtful that Jim would have been able to make it through more than two or three takes...

Been Down So Long, a stomping blues in the old Doors manner, shows up Jim's vocal problems even more clearly, with his having to resort to out and out shouting in places; nonetheless, it's a fresh driving track which works by virtue of its very roughness. The lyric of *Cars Hiss By My Window* dates back to Jim's Venice days and the song is taken along at a lazy slope by Jerry Scheff's bass, with a slight delay on Jim's doubled vocal glossing over the rough corners.

The WASP shares with *Changeling* a 1968 genesis, but there all similarity ends, for where the latter is unusually accessible for a song of that period, the former contains its allotted quota of Morrisonian lines and more than its fair share of Jim rapping. For a song that changes pace almost every other bar, it holds together well and also contains one of the earliest uses of synthesised drumming, which John develops only briefly, but to great effect. *L'America* was originally recorded for Michelangelo Antonioni's 1969 film *Zabriskie Point*, a somewhat confused and confusing allegory of contemporary America which also featured music by Pink Floyd, the Grateful Dead and Kaleidoscope, among others. The piece swings from blues strut to 'old' Doors before assuming a quasi-Floydian weirdness. Once again, thanks to a

sympathetic production, Jim sounds almost up to snuff.

On *Morrison Hotel*, the convention of having one long cut per album had lapsed, an omission which *L.A. Woman* rectified by closing each side with a seven minute plus track. The title cut is a classic cruising song, and indeed opens with a driving bass line, soon joined by a tack piano and Robbie's guitar, commenting on Jim's rough yet fitting vocal. *L.A. Woman* is in essence a lighter sequel to *The Soft Parade*, both songs being scrapbook cameos of Los Angeles, the former from the outside, the latter the view of someone who's lived in the city perhaps a little *too* long... The power of the building *Mr. Mojo Risin'* segment is particularly notable and the subsequent return to the opening phrase gives the song a cyclical structure and an innate unity unusual for a song of its length.

Riders On The Storm, the album's closer, is possessed of a quiet intensity not evident on first hearing. A feature obvious from the very first note, however, is a full return to the 'old' Doors menacing yet cosy atmosphere, an effect heightened by the use of a whispered double track and thunderstorm effects opening and closing the song. An image from Jim's *HWY* film surfaces in the second verse and elsewhere autobiographical elements appear, giving the song an air of being something of a final statement and, by virtue of its placement on the album, investing the remainder of the LP with a similar feeling, a tenet Doors chronicler Jerry Hopkins supports.

"With L.A. Woman, *there was nothing further that Jim had to do to satisfy anyone in terms of album production, and he thought that that would be a perfect opportunity to get away from Los Angeles."*

With the release of *L.A. Woman*, the Doors' contractual commitment was fulfilled and, whilst relations between the record company and the band weren't as cordial as they had been, there was no reason for anyone to think that they wouldn't be re-signed. However, despite the myriad changes the band had been through, at least one factor had re-

89

mained constant, and that was the unwritten understanding that the band was a working democracy, as a result of which any re-signing would be postponed until Jim returned from Paris. Gossip being what it is, however, the word rapidly spread that the Doors were leaving Elektra. A year or two previously, the prevailing feeling would have been along the lines of 'interesting – but are they worth the trouble involved ?' However, the success of the single and the album had not gone unnoticed, and major companies such as Atlantic and Columbia were reported to have made approaches. How serious these overtures may have been, and how the band regarded them, is now a point for conjecture, for there's no hard evidence that the Doors were planning to leave Elektra. If so, would Max Fink have continued discussions with the company regarding Jim's poetry album? As for the others, Ray recalls that

> "we'd rehearse every once in a while... maybe get together twice a week, working on some songs and stuff, and just waiting for Jim to come back."

Jim, in the meantime, was finding the reality of creative exile in Paris somewhat different from what he had expected, and for this only really had himself to blame, for he was still drinking very heavily, as Doors biographer Hervé Muller remembers.

> "He was drunk a lot... that's not to say I never saw him sober, but it usually didn't last,"

a condition due in no small part to the profusion of sidewalk bars and cafés open round the clock. It was in one of these, the Astroquet, that Jim met an American singer called Phil Trainer, who later wrote a song about him called *Beautiful Jim*. Interestingly, Trainer failed to recognise Jim straight away, which rather contradicts Danny Sugerman's opinion that

> "He (Jim) was almost as famous in Paris as he was in Los Angeles, and he really couldn't get away from being Jim Morrison, rock star, singer of the Doors".

Strange, then, that an American in Paris took some time to register who he was drinking with... Hervé Muller noted

> "Sometimes he was recognised, sometimes

not, and he didn't really mind either way." Not surprisingly, the object of the Parisian trip – to concentrate on his poetry – suffered accordingly, with little, if any, new material forthcoming. In Hervé Muller's opinion,

> "I don't think he was doing anything. I didn't have a lot to do with that side, but while he was in Paris, I don't think he was doing much. He had his notebooks and things with him and he was making notes, but I didn't see him working. Maybe he did, but..."

The situation had the makings of a classic vicious circle; because of the drinking, the poetry suffered, which depressed Jim, something he fought with drink... and so on. To break out of this apparently downward spiral, Jim and Pam took a couple of longish side trips, spending three weeks in April and May touring France, Spain and Morocco and a further ten days at the end of May in Corsica.

Jim apparently phoned back to Los Angeles twice, once to tell the Doors manager Bill Siddons that he needed a little while longer before coming back, and once to ask John Densmore how things were going. His surprise at learning how well *L.A. Woman* and the singles from it were doing could well be related to Hervé Muller's recollection of Jim's musical attitude at the time;

> "He'd left the band, as far as he was concerned, at that point. That doesn't mean he might not have recorded with them again – he wasn't the kind of guy who would think ahead too much."

Throughout the month of June, it appears that Jim worked in a somewhat desultory manner on his extra-musical concerns; he'd brought copies of *Feast Of Friends* and *HWY* to Paris with him and tried on odd occasions to arrange screenings, but without success. As ever, there were talks concerning varied and nebulous film projects, and attempts at producing something worthwhile in the poetry line, but again with little apparent success. It wasn't that Jim had lost any of his interest – in fact, his last communication with the United States was a request to his publishers, asking that they drop the intended cover photograph for the paperback edition of *The Lords & The New Creatures* (taken in the late

1960s) and use a more recent shot – but that the words simply wouldn't come, despite Jim's attempts to clear his head by going on the wagon.

The last time anyone reliable (that is, anyone apart from Pam) saw Jim alive was on the evening of Friday, July 2nd, when he, Pam and Alan Ronay met for a meal close by Jim's residence at the time. Ronay remembers Jim as being exceedingly depressed and recommended a Robert Mitchum film, *Pursued*, knowing that Jim admired the actor. Jim apparently decided to go and see the movie, took Pam back home and set off for the cinema alone. From this point on hard facts become a rare commodity whilst rumours abound... and by Monday morning, the rumours were that Jim had died at some unspecified time over the weekend. For reasons never adequately explained, it was the British national press who first broke the story, phoning Elektra Records in London for confirmation who, in turn contacted the company's Paris offices, only to learn that Elektra, France, hadn't even known of Jim's presence in the city! Calls to the US Embassy and Paris police revealed that no American named Morrison had shown up at any city morgue.

In the interim, however, a couple of the UK rock weeklies had also called Elektra for news concerning the Morrison rumours implying that if the rock press, with their widespread and deep-rooted contacts, were taking the matter seriously...

When the phone woke Bill Siddons and he'd digested the essence of the call, his initial reaction was probably "not again", for during the late sixties, Jim passed on with monotonous regularity almost each weekend. It had become something of a standing joke about the Doors Office, Bill greeting Jim on Monday with "You're supposed to be dead, you know," to which Jim's stock reply was "Again – how'd I go *this* time?" Nonetheless, if a transatlantic call had been considered necessary, it might not hurt just to check with the man himself, so Siddons dialled Jim's Paris number, fully expecting to hear him at the other end. What he actually got was Pam, telling him he'd best come right

CHRIS WALTER PHOTOFEATURES INT.

91

over, but apparently refusing to be more explicit. The possibility of a long distance leg-pull crossed his mind – Pam had never been that fond of Siddons – but he took the next available flight, reasoning that if *she* wanted him in Paris, something had to be up.

Upon arriving on Tuesday the 6th, Siddons went straight to the flat, where he discovered Pam, a sealed coffin and a death certificate giving the cause of Jim's death as a heart attack induced by respiratory problems. The following afternoon, the coffin was interred at Père LaChaise cemetery. On the Thursday, Siddons and Pam returned to Los Angeles and on Friday, Siddons issued a press release, detailing the events of the weekend as related to him by Pam.

According to her, Jim had returned to the flat early on Saturday morning (presumably after seeing the movie) and, after coughing up a small amount of blood, said he felt like a bath. After dropping off to sleep, Pam woke at five, to find Jim still in the bath, apparently asleep. Her initial thought that Jim was staging a black joke vanished when she failed to rouse him and called the Parisian equivalent of a para-medic unit, who apparently arrived with the police and a doctor in tow, the latter pronouncing Jim dead. That was all.

For a statement presumably designed to quash any incipient rumours that must inevitably accompany such an event, it was wholly unsuccessful, one major bone of contention being that it had taken some six days for the 'official' story to be made public, ample time for a cover story to be concocted. A glaring inconsistency is Pam's assertion that the police were in attendance on the Saturday Jim's death allegedly took place. That was July 3rd, yet when Elektra UK phoned the Paris police two days later, they were told that no-one answering Jim's name or description had died over the weekend. It may appear suspicious, or at the very least strange that, some forty-eight hours after Jim's alleged time of death, his demise hadn't been filed *somewhere*, especially as the police were alleged to have been involved from the beginning – but it must be remembered that,

92 no matter where it happened, the wheels of

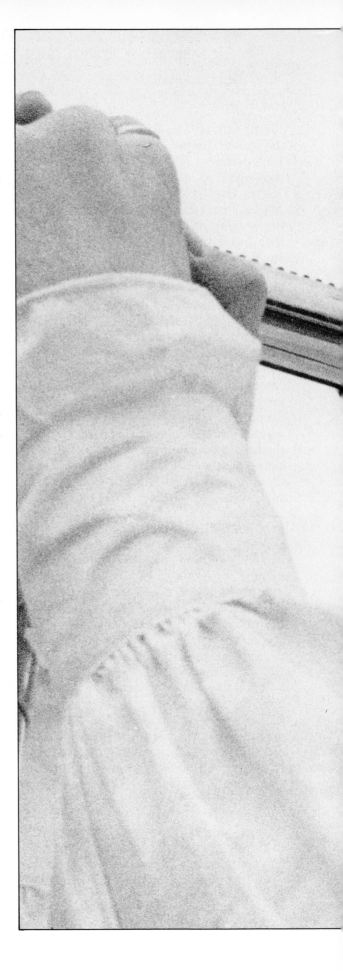

bureaucracy tend to grind exceedingly slow. The cause of death was similarly held up for examination, and generally found to be wanting. The overwhelming feeling was that the last thing Jim might die of would be either old age or a heart attack. The vague mention of a respiratory factor being a problem also baffled; true, he had twice suffered from pneumonia (which apparently went untreated), but that was some two years previously and, according to those who knew him in Paris, Jim was – drinking aside – enjoying rather better health than he had for some time. Phil Trainer had observed that Jim suffered from a heavy smoker's cough... but then so do many people in worse shape than Jim was but they don't croak in the bath.

The lack of an autopsy – strange in the case of so sudden and apparently unexpected a demise – and the continuing anonymity of the attending doctor also serve to raise the collective eyebrow at the 'official' account. Needless to say, underground rumours abounded, some – if not most – of which strained credulity to its limits. One, however, holds water better than most and supposes that Jim, either instead of, or after, seeing the movie Ronay suggested, visited the Circus, a Paris club where he had become a regular, which also doubled as the local heroin centre, and accidentally overdosed on the drug in an effort to shake off his increasing depression. A flaw in this notion is that it's highly unlikely that Jim injected the drug as he had an almost pathological fear of hypodermic needles. On the other hand, if he'd snorted the drug and had been drinking (a not unlikely supposition), the facts fit. The quantity of ingested heroin reckoned to be lethal is considerably lowered by the presence of alcohol in the bloodstream, the two drugs combining to knock out the nervous and breathing mechanisms to bring about a quick and pain-free death... and a bath is the usual place for the attempted revival of a heroin overdose, though why is something of a poser; there appears to be no sound medical reason for such a treatment. Another generally accepted rumour is that Pam wasn't with Jim that weekend and only discovered him

when she returned on the Monday; this is more plausible as it accounts for the delay in issuing the statement and the inconsistencies therein.

The fact of the matter is that no-one can be certain how Jim died; as Hervé Muller says,

"There's a mystery about the way he died, but there's no mystery about his being dead."

This second observation moves the Morrison Death Mystery into its secondary and less believable phase, the one that holds that Jim *isn't* dead but had staged everything in order to drop out of being a public figure. The central piece of evidence for this theory is the admittedly undeniable fact that nobody who can be traced actually saw the body, nor does it appear that any accounts of what happened to Jim's corpse over the weekend (assuming he did die on the Saturday) have come to light. This, however, tends to throw more doubt on his time of death than anything else, but he must have been kept in reasonably cold conditions somewhere and, if Pam is to be believed over the police presence, the police morgue would be the logical answer... but there's apparently no record. One ingenious theory, put forward by a noted rock writer who should really know better, postulated that Jim had dropped out of sight in order to let any statute of limitations pertaining to the Miami trial expire, after which time he would return a free man and pick up the threads (and royalties...). The surviving Doors have always presented a unified front when questioned and a 1977 interview with John outlines the 'party-line' as neatly as any;

"I saw Pamela a few months afterwards and when I looked into her eyes I felt pretty much that Jim was dead... on the other hand, he's just about the only person I've met in my whole life who was wild enough to pull a fast one like that – he was wild enough to go to the Greek Islands and not tell anybody."

Except Pam, of course, for if there was any plot to vanish she *must* have been party to it. As she succumbed to a fatal overdose herself in the spring of 1974, having said nothing decisive one way or the other, the possibility is always there, however faint. There is, however, one tiny thing she said which could be used to counter the 'still-alive' protagonists.

"Jim's spirit often left his body and he returned from magical cities with strange tales to tell", she said, then added *"This time he didn't come back... that's all."*

Needless to say, there have been sightings of 'Jim' down the years, centering in the main around San Francisco and, as John noted, the Greek Islands. There's the story of 'Jim' suddenly appearing at the doorstep of an obscure Mid-West radio station in the dead of night and doing a long interview explaining it all before vanishing into the darkness again. Needless to say, no tapes were made and no-one can remember hearing the show, hence the whole tale has a more than dubious ring to it... and, of course, there's *Phantom's Divine Comedy*, an LP released in 1974 on Capitol Records with the enigmatic credits "drums & percussion, X: bass, Y & W; piano & organ, Z: vocals, guitar & piano, Phantom". The front slick was an out-of-focus colour negative shot which suggested that if it was Jim, he'd had radical bone surgery on his cheeks. Certainly, the vocal on the first song was close enough to make even a sceptic think twice, but those claiming it *was* Jim obviously hadn't listened any further, for the voice soon assumes the tone and phrasing of any competent American hard rock vocalist. Perhaps the most interesting point about this bizarre release is that never once was it claimed by anyone actually connected with the disc that it was Jim; it was just released and the listeners made up their own minds...

When someone attains Jim's popularity and notoriety, there will always be those who will elevate the object of their adulation above mere mortal status. Perhaps, as recently happened with Lee Harvey Oswald, the only answer is to open the grave in Père LaChaise with a copy of Jim's dental charts to hand. Until then, there will always be adherents to the 'he's-still-around' cause but taking into account all the evidence, facts and plausible rumours, there's little doubt there *was* a body in the coffin interred on July 7th, 1971, in Paris and equally little doubt that the body *was* that of James Douglas Morrison, would-be film maker, published poet, on his night an amazing frontman and, ultimately, one of a string of rock 'n' roll casualities.

JIM MARSHALL

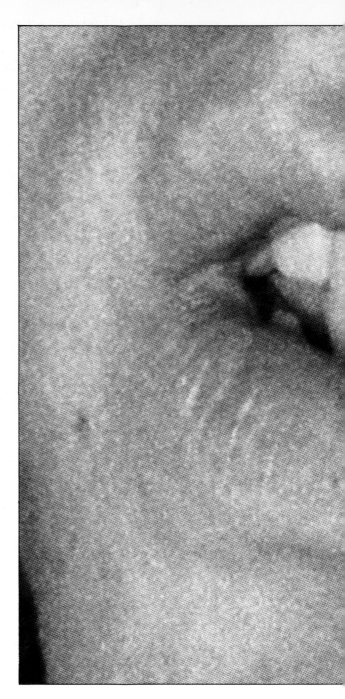

"*When we received the news from Paris about Jim,*" said John Densmore in late 1971, "*we were shocked beyond belief. That really did it... we just thought 'What now?' We sat around, and then we jammed a bit, and finally we decided to keep the music going, keep on making music. The vibes between the three of us had been so good that we felt we just had to continue. Jim was a friend, somebody you'd lived with and made music with for so long, but eventually we began to realise that we had the rest of our lives to live, so after we'd gotten over it, we started to think about what we'd do. None of us really wanted to go play with anyone else, so after five years of being together and getting tighter, we decided to start the whole thing again.*"

John's comment about starting the whole thing over may seem a little puzzling until pulled into sharp focus by an observation from Ray, dating from roughly the same time;

"*The important thing was always music, and there were so many things fighting against it that we decided to... quit for a while, lay low. Jim was fed up with*

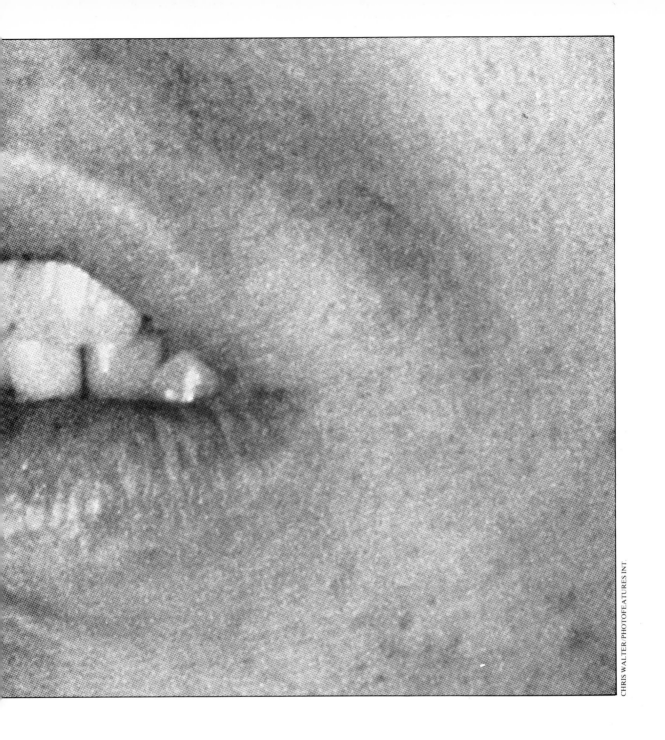

everything and just wanted to go away and write. So, effectively, by the time he went to Paris, the Doors were not talking in group terms anymore... we were all kinda tired of being Doors."

Robbie agrees that

"It was all very much up in the air as to what we were going to do."

Not, it would appear, for too long, however... or perhaps it was that Jim's untimely – though perhaps not completely unexpected – departure galvanised the remaining members into action, returning to the Doors Workshop in late July to develop a number of the post *L.A. Woman* jams into material for a new album, for which the band had re-signed to Elektra for a further three years. But before heading studiowards, there were two important decisions to be made. Firstly, the name:

"We were going to change it. We had thought about changing it, but nobody could come up with anything that didn't sound really pretentious."

remembers Robbie. Ray, tongue planted firmly in cheek, adds

"We even thought of calling ourselves 'And The Doors', because at the beginning it was 'The Doors', then after a few years it was 'Jim Morrison and the Doors' so... But we kept 'The Doors' because that's who we still are; there were four of us – now there are three of us."

The other consideration was inevitable and caused a certain amount of speculation within the rock world.

"Yes, we thought about finding another singer, but it seemed kinda impossible to bring in another personality. We'd been together so long, the four of us, that the psychic communication was so strong that it would take a long time to adapt and harmonise to a new guy... and what if he's not the right guy? And of course, it would really be hard on the guy, too, because he'd always be Jim's replacement."

Thus it was that when the Doors returned to the studio, again in the company of co-producer Bruce Botnick, the chore of lead vocalist in general fell to Ray, with Robbie taking a couple of leads and generally harmo-

nising. Initially, the indecision at what to do after Jim's death carried over to the sessions, as Ray recalled:

"At first, we were very unsure of ourselves... we didn't exactly know what we were going to sound like. We knew that the music would be OK, but we weren't too sure about the vocals, how they were gonna sound. We just didn't know how it was going to gel... but, little by little, it began falling together..."

Helped, no doubt, by having some tracks left over from *L.A. Woman. Down On The Farm* was a song Jim had rejected during his last sessions in LA, and it seems logical to assume that the other two songs featuring Jerry Scheff on bass date from the same period. John confirms that

"A couple of the songs had been around for a year or so, but the rest are new... they might be songs we'd sort of thought of doing, but it wasn't right then."

which seems a reasonable indication that Jim and the Doors were, in fact, drifting apart, if only musically.

The bulk of the tracks were recorded during August and September 1971, with a host of supplementary musicians – on bass, aside from Scheff, Jack Conrad, Ray Neapolitan (who was the bassist for most of *Morrison Hotel*, so it's possible that the basic track for *Ships w/ Sails* dates from then), Willie Ruff and Wolfgang Meltz, percussionist Francisco Aguabella, a definite character who John remembers as having purple congas and not speaking English, whilst Ray recalls,

"His drums looked like 1958 Cadillacs, with big fins and everything!",

whilst Emil Richards is credited with supplying marimba, kickshaws and whimwhams. Marimba – fair enough... but the other two? Ray elucidates:

"A kickshaw or a whimwham is an archaic American term for little things clanking, knick-knacks, anything that makes a noise. Emil probably has the world's largest collection of them, and he travels all over the world with them, and African and ethnic instruments as well. He's a standard LA jazz figure, been

around for quite a while, played with Paul Horn... Most of the music you've heard in the big movies like 2001, *all the weird sounds, are probably him."*

The album, entitled – with quiet humour – *Other Voices*, was released towards the end of October and was handled with extreme caution by fans and reviewers alike, with some justification. Were this the debut album from a totally new band, it would undoubtedly have received a fairer hearing... but this is the Doors and, there's the nagging feeling that, secure in the knowledge that the long-standing fans would buy the album anyway, either out of loyalty or curiosity, Ray, Robbie and John perhaps eased up on the creativity and explored a few too many avenues, resulting in a generally inconclusive album musically. Of the eight tracks, half are of some vintage, and it would not be unfair to say that these are, in general, the better cuts. *Ships w/ Sails* showcases best the 'old' Doors sparse-yet-warm sound, wedded to an almost Dave Brubeck style rhythm. All the old hallmarks are there – a cyclic structure, workable instrumental break (although the attempt to emulate a *Light My Fire* climax doesn't quite come off) and excellent guitar from Robbie. It's almost as if the band was reluctant to leave the ground they'd known so long, despite assertions in the press that the post-Morrison material was "a further extension", a point highlighted by Ray attempting, and pulling off, a passable imitation of Jim's phrasing. It's easily the best vocal performance on the album, but hard on its heels comes evidence that Ray had more than a little trouble with the lower register.

As with *Ships w/ Sails*, the subtle influence of J.D. Morrison is detectable on the first three songs of side two. As noted before, Jim had decided against including *Down On The Farm* on *L.A. Woman*, probably due to the song's middle eight, which is reminiscent of the chorus from *Runnin' Blue*. This aside, the track passes muster as a good, second division Doors song. *I'm Horny, I'm Stoned* as a title gives this song a good head start and together with a stomping tack piano intro and Robbie's fluid guitar lines leading into an all out fun singalong track, the number can be taken as a catalogue of life in the Doors, or in the days of hippiedom generally. Again, there is a vague countrified feeling but this time Robbie pulls it off with great panache. Whilst *Horny/Stoned* could be considered Jim's theme song, *Wandering Musician* could equally be said to be a song for Jim – as indeed Ray once said it was – and, indirectly, the Doors' own tribute to him. Although the instrumental break never really gets going the remainder of the song is more than acceptable. The closing track, *Hang Onto Your Life* – aside from having what could be considered a somewhat tasteless title – would appear to be one of the newer, truly post-Jim tracks and demonstrated the extent of the indecision and lack of direction within the band. To the casual ear, it might appear to be segments of some three disparate songs spliced together at random; opening with an 'old Doors'-ish figure overlaid with a jazzy guitar riff from Robbie, it changes to a chorus sounding more like Crosby, Stills, Nash & Young than C, S, N & Y and then becomes a weird and frantic closing segment. Opening the album, *In The Eye Of The Sun* sounds not unlike a sequel to *Riders On The Storm* with a jazzy Doors strut and loose drums setting the tone for a Morrisonesque lyric and typically sparse guitar from Robbie behind the verses. His solo, a little further into the song, is, however, the equal of anything he'd previously done. The final wince-worthy line, however "So I thought up the world/And you did too" – almost manages to undo all the preceding good work. *Variety Is The Spice Of Life* is pretty much your standard Krieger, with some great multi-tracked guitars in mid-song and, just to balance the scales, some rather dubious rhymes in the middle-eight. Closing side one is easily the best of the newer songs, *Tightrope Ride*, a straight ahead thrash with few frills, Robbie's best guitar of the entire album and a gritty, fitting vocal from Ray. It came as no surprise, therefore, when this track was chosen as the single from the album, reaching number seventy-one in America.

Other Voices fared rather better, hitting thirty-one in the US album charts, and taking everything into consideration, both album

99

and single did rather better than could reasonably have been expected, for although the musicianship is, as ever, faultless, the vocals are a cause for concern. The principle behind not replacing Jim, as previously outlined, was doubtless laudable... however, that was not really the point. The band needed something extra. On *L.A. Woman*, Jim's voice may have been on the way out, but it retained some of its depth and presence; Ray (and to a lesser extent Robbie) are simply... there. *Rolling Stone* probably hit the mark when it observed

> *"It is Doors music mainly due to its trappings... they are still the Doors but without a cause or passion; it is obvious that Jim Morrison was more than just a singer..."*

It was with such media opinions lurking in the back of their minds that the Doors decided to take to the road again, both to promote the new product *and* to demonstrate that the Doors minus Morrison didn't, of necessity, spell disaster. To enable them to reproduce the album live, two supplementary musicians were recruited; on bass, Jack Conrad, who had in fact toured with the Doors before and who, according to John,

> *"worked with Helen Reddy and writes a lot of stuff with her... had some hits on the charts"*

and on rhythm guitar and assorted percussion, Bobby Ray, of whom Robbie recalls

> *"He was an old friend of ours from L.A. He'd played bass with Donovan on* Sunshine Superman, *and had played bass on the road with the Mamas and Papas. I'd known him for quite a while, and he'd toured with us before. The summer after he came with us, he put out a solo album,* Initiation Of The Mystic... *I think Johnny Rivers produced it."*

The tour had a less than auspicious beginning, with dates in Toronto and Ottawa pulling very small crowds. By the time the Doors reached New York's Carnegie Hall (via the likes of Lincoln, Nebraska and Philadelphia), it was standing room only, and all along the line, the reviews had been universal in their praise of the concerts. It was evident that not only did the *Other Voices* material work better live (the only LP track omitted was *Wandering Musician*), but that, as with the 'old' Doors, the band itself was a different entity on stage. The crowds tended to agree with the critics, though again there were doubtless a fair number of the curious salted amongst the faithful; this audience reaction was all the more surprising (and satisfying) because, the new album aside, the only other songs performed were *Love Me Two Times, Close To You, Good Rockin' Tonight* (the old Elvis number) and, of course, *Light My Fire*. Whilst the audiences (naturally) acclaimed the golden oldies, they also reacted favourably towards the newer material, dispelling Ray's slight reservations:

> *"I think it's going to take people a little while to adjust to what we're doing. At first, I think it might be rather confusing for them... but little by little, if they'll just listen and dig the music..."*

In January 1972, as the Doors began rehearsing titles for a new album, and for an upcoming European tour in the spring, Elektra cast an eye over the back catalogue and decided a little more repackaging was in order, hence the appearance of *Weird Scenes Inside The Goldmine*. This double set was notable only in that it was a perfect complement to the earlier compilation, *13*, including several very long cuts, and in the inclusion of two songs – *Who Scared You* and *(You Need Meat) Don't Go No Further* – previously available only as B sides. As a commercial venture, it was successful enough and reached number fifty five in the charts. As an albeit unwitting first step in keeping the memory of Jim Morrison alive, it was an even greater success.

The Doors' second European tour, spanning April and May, saw them play in Germany, Switzerland, France, Belgium, Holland and the UK before winding up the trip with a return visit to the Roundhouse... which would have been nice had it happened, but in the event, the last UK gig was switched to the Imperial College, London. No matter, as the music was once again right up to snuff and the 'new' Doors – once again accompanied by Jack Conrad and Bobby Ray. – impressed the fans and critics easily as much as the 'old' Doors. As the band flew back to the States to commence sessions for the new album, two tracks of which had been premiered in Europe, their future looked, if not precisely rosy, at least assured, and there was no means of knowing that the Imperial College gig was to be the absolute swansong of the performing Doors...

Once back in Los Angeles, the recording of a new album commenced, the process being transferred from the Doors' Workshop to the A & M studios in Hollywood and co-producer/engineer Bruck Botnick being gently dropped in the move. Jack Conrad was retained for bass duties in three songs and played rhythm guitar on another, whilst the remaining bass chores were split between Chris Ethridge, Charles Larkey and Leland Sklar, all notable session players. Additional musicians were percussionists Bobbi Hall and Chico Batera and veteran jazz man Charles Lloyd on sax and flute (a billing which must have given Doors fans considerable pause for thought – sax and flute on a *Doors* album?), the ensemble being rounded off by the backing vocalists Clydie King, Melissa Mackay and Venetta Fields. Though Lloyd was a jazzer of some note, with umpteen albums to his name (including *Live In Russia!*) his ventures into the rock field had been limited to a mediocre Transcendental Meditation inspired album *Warm Waters* and contributions to various Beach Boys songs of the early seventies, thus his rock credentials could be considered tenuous at best.

As it transpired, the release of *Full Circle* demonstrated that it was for his jazz pedigree that Lloyd had been invited to contribute. The LP also underlined the band's continuing indecision. On *Other Voices* the writing credits assigned all songs to the Doors, whereas on *Full Circle*, individual song credits were the order of the day, and it's tempting to suppose that this was because, as per *Soft Parade*, someone didn't want it thought they had contributed to such and such a track. As before, the album suffers from vocals ranging from the acceptable to the decidedly dubious; equally as before, the

musicianship on all the tracks is up to the usual Doors standard (that is, impeccable). Unfortunately, the material is more often than not as dubious as the vocals, not helped by a substandard production.

As ever, the LP opens with a traditional Doors rocker, *Get Up And Dance*, which comes over almost as a gospel track due in the main to the backing vocals and handclaps, not to mention a vaguely inspirational lyric. A similarly nebulous/mystical lyric almost takes the edge off Robbie's *Four Billion Souls*, but the typical Krieger bar-room attack emerges the winner assisted by John's excellent drumming and a good organ/guitar interplay during the middle eight.

Verdilac is the first stumbling block (en passant, what *is* a verdilac? The word doesn't apparently exist in any dictionary...). A muddled opening detracts from a rather fine ensuing Doors-cum-jazz stroll, which itself is negated by superfluous sax intrusion and a vocal which immediately jars. The instrumental passage meanders in a way that no 'old' Doors long track ever did, although there's some nice guitar from Robbie counteracting some more soporific sax. The spoken Transcendental Meditation section that follows is, frankly, acutely embarrassing and is strong evidence that Mike Love of the Beach Boys isn't alone in writing truly duff TM songs. The closing aside raises a smile, albeit mostly from relief. Further relief is to hand in the form of *Hardwood Floor*, more bar room Krieger which swings along nicely with Ray's vocal fitting perfectly, the whole song generally exuding more energy than the previous three tracks put together. *Good Rockin'* is possibly the most polished studio jam ever committed to wax and is none the worse for that, though Ray's vocal, thin to begin with, tends towards parody as the song progresses. Robbie plays his way through the Scotty Moore songbook in inimitable style and the track generally is – except perhaps to Elvis purists – more than acceptable.

The Mosquito is another track completely killed by a very, very poor intro, from which it never recovers despite excellent guitar work from Robbie; another aimless meander with a handful of interesting musical ideas, but not sufficient to last the song's five minutes plus length. *Piano Bird* just isn't the Doors – it sounds more like Santana and one doubts if anyone would care to admit to having penned the lyric, which is irredeemably lame... as is, sad to say, the lyric of the following track, *It Slipped My Mind*, a repetitive song with a less than top notch vocal.

Side two of *Full Circle* is saved from being a full-scale disaster by the closing track, *The Peking King And The New York Queen* which wins through almost in spite of a storyline which sets out describing an extra-terrestrial visitation and wanders through an East vs. West spoken section which is vaguely insulting (and definitely irritating) before ending up as a more or less political statement. Once again, the musical cavalry rides over the horizon to the rescue, imbuing the track with a passing likeness to *The Soft Parade*, most notably during the intro and following the East/West dialogue.

It has been said, perhaps unkindly, that the most interesting aspect of *Full Circle* was the elaborate packaging, which included a press-out-and-assemble-yourself zoetrope, illustrating the 'circle of life' theme on the sleeve. Be that as it may, it was obvious that the album highlighted several problems which the band has previously considered solved, or had gently ignored. John recalls that:

> *"In retrospect,* Full Circle *was a bit of a disaster, but at the time we had our hearts in it. Then, about halfway through, the songwriting thing started to get on everyone's nerves... Which song are we going to do, Ray's turning this way, Robbie that way, so it all got a little touchy, which is why I don't think the album turned out that well."*

In addition to internal problems came the realisation that the need for someone who could really sing was paramount. Whilst these matters were being considered, both the album and the single taken from it, *The Mosquito*, were making brief appearances in the lower reaches of the Hot 100; the single peaked at 85* whilst the album topped out at 68, really rather fine showings considering

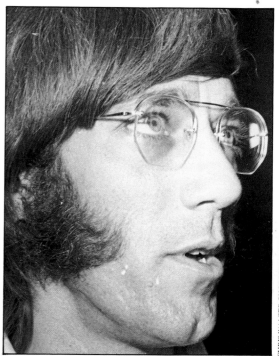

*In the UK, the 45 was *Get Up and Dance*, backed with an album out-take, *Tree Trunks*.

the weakness of the material and the critical and public disfavour the band was now inevitably attracting.

The quest for a new singer resulted in the Doors travelling to London in the fall of 1972 to audition new blood, a wonderfully illogical move when one considers that, at the time, Los Angeles was unquestionably the musical capital of the world. Ray is, for once, decidedly brief about the venture:

> "We wanted to recharge our creative batteries, just as Jim did when he went to Paris... but it didn't really work out. It was time to close the Doors."

John, however, is more specific:

> "We came over to London to find a vocalist, and as we started jamming with various singers, we realised more than ever that when you have a good, professional singer who can do with his voice what someone else could do with their instrument, how much more fluent everything is... but that led to the writing problems. Everyone, myself included, was writing songs, and all of Ray's were real personal, and so it finally got to the point where it was obvious that he was the only one who could sing them, because they'd be very philosophical and cosmic or whatever, so how could another singer relate to material that was so personal? So, when we first came over, we were still together – sort of – but when we realised how very differently our musical directions were heading, Ray split back home. Then Robbie and I decided that, as we'd come over to start something new, we might as well do it anyway, and so for the next four months or so, we lived here and jammed with different people, and eventually sorted something out."

Nothing is that straightforward, and Robbie remembers that

> "It wasn't very easy. You call up people and say 'Come down and jam', but they'd know it was really an audition and the pressure would creep in..."

The 'auditions' spanned the Christmas/New Year period 1972/3 and, the fates displayed a fine sense of irony, a singer was the first new member recruited to the as yet un-named band. John:

> "Jess Roden was the first; we'd been through a few singers, but Jess seemed right. He sang Robbie's melodies well and he had some of his own material."

Prior to meeting Robbie and John, Roden had established a reputation as a fine singer, firstly with Alan Bown before forming Bronco. At the time of the auditions, he was doing sessions for the likes of the Who and Paul Kossoff, Bronco having foundered.

It was through Roden that the final pair of recruits were acquired;

> "Jess brought Philip and Roy with him. Philip's a really excellent bass player – we went through a lot of bass players, and then he came in and played. Didn't even start a song; he played for about ten seconds and Robbie and I looked at each other and said, 'This is it!'"

Chen was a well known session bassist, with a track record dating back to a 1966 Jimmy James & the Vagabonds LP and embracing in the process such diverse talents as Linda Lewis, Donovan, Jeff Beck and, in later years, Rod Stewart, Joan Armatrading, Jim Capaldi and stage appearances with the New Barbarians, Keith Richards' 'parole' band following one of his drug busts.

> "Roy Davies was in this band called Gonzalez", as John remembers, "which had fifteen or twenty members... like they had two or three drummers, bass players, whatever, and whenever someone can't make it, one of the others stands in. Just a local band of really good players."★

Roy Davies had to ward off competition for the keyboard slot, in the form of Mick Weaver (ex-Traffic, or to be more accurate, ex-Mason, Capaldi, Wood and Frog for, when Weaver replaced Steve Winwood, he adopted for reasons best known to himself the handle of Wynder K. Frog) but as John observed at the time,

> "I don't think Mick was to be in the band, and he knew it too... but he did a couple of sessions with us all the same."

★Roy never really 'left' Gonzalez, his keyboards being one of the few stable factors through some seven years and six albums, one of which, *Haven't Stopped Dancing*, contained the hit single of the same name.

For several months in early 1973, the Butts Band – perhaps named after an area of countryside just outside Brighton, Sussex – began recording their debut album for Blue Thumb Records. This wasn't the original intent, as John explains;

> *"We were in the process of signing, or rather thinking about signing the Butts Band to Elektra, because of Jac Holzman.*
>
> *As the Doors, we had had a fairly good relationship with him over the years – he was a sort of friend and father figure... but he decided to retire, so he was up and gone and we were out on the street. The original notion was to be on Elektra in the States and Island in the UK, but with Jac pulling out the rug and going, things changed around quite a bit. Then we remembered Bob Krasnow of Blue Thumb; he'd sort of been in the background all along, liked the band and was really enthusiastic – it wasn't money, really, he was just very committed."*

The eventual upshot was that the album would be released on Blue Thumb in the UK, but distributed by Island.

Sessions for the album were well underway at Olympic studios in London when the entire band upped and left to complete the project in Kingston, Jamaica. Whether or not this was always part of the plan, or merely a spur-of-the-moment notion, has never been too clear: the nearest approach to an explanation came from John in a press release;

> *"We chose Jamaica because of the reggae music which surrounds you in that country. You hear reggae blasting from every open door, and it's a different, exciting rhythm. Our music might not be reggae, but the influence is there and it's a great help in shaping our direction."*

As a solid reason for doing a London/Jamaican split, such a statement leaves a little to be desired, especially as shortly after the album's release, John had a swift re-think and announced

> *"We're not really that reggae influenced, that's been blown out of all proportion. It's*

just that Phil was born there... I think we're more a white soul band than a reggae thing... and I don't think it sounds like the Doors either. While we were making the album I couldn't really be objective, but now I don't think it sounds like the Doors beyond that the guitarist and drummer are from the Doors. Robbie and I have been influenced by different stuff now, and I think it's going to go further away. It feels good to do something new, to be done with the Doors – it was great, believe me, but it's fresh now, and exciting to have to start all over and have to scuffle around."

Jess Roden, not unnaturally, offers a different slant on things.

> *"The first thing we did was to rehearse for a few weeks and then go and record an album, which struck me as a bad idea, not having played live or anything. Elektra were quite interested initially; Jac Holzman said he'd definitely sign the band, but he copped out and handed the matter over to David Geffen, who didn't like us and therefore didn't sign us. So that was three months of the band's life wasted, and it brought the English contingent down no end; we thought, 'No way is this going to work.' Then they came up with the idea of us all living in America to try to consolidate things, and I decided I wasn't gonna live in the US, no way."*

The debut album, entitled with breathtaking originality *The Butts Band*, certainly wasn't the Doors nor anything like true reggae. Nor, truth to tell, was it anything really new as far as the music scene of 1974 was concerned, and in the annals of rock, the years 1971 to 1975 were probably the most musically stagnant since 1959. Therefore, by association, whilst pleasant enough to the ear *The Butts Band* didn't exactly set the world alight. Of the two sides, the one recorded in Jamaica is the more lively, with the opener, *Won't Be Alone Anymore*, contriving to sound decidedly Monkee-ish whilst setting the general tenor of the LP – excellent guitar (as ever) from Robbie, though more to the fore than had previously been the case, precise drumming from John and workmanlike vocals from Jess Roden more than compensating for the short-comings on the final pair of Doors LPs. *Baja Bus* gives the impression of being a *Full Circle* left over, whilst Jess Roden's *Sweet Danger* exudes a decidedly latter day Crosby, Stills, Nash and Young air with which Roy Davies mingles a few organ lines lifted directly from *Riders On The Storm*. *Pop-A-Top...* well the best thing about it is Robbie's bottleneck; otherwise, it's something of a wasted track.

The London side never really escapes from a laid-back groove and in fact, until the final track, it tends to plod. The closer, *Kansas City*, the old Leiber and Stoller classic, is something of a curio, for it's not the stage track it purports to be. True, it was recorded in one take at Olympic studios, but the crowd response was dubbed over at a later date, a move Jess Roden took a somewhat dim view of.

"I think they took the applause off an old Doors album or something and I wasn't too pleased with that."

In fact, in Britain, the Butts Band appeared in concert just once, supporting the Kinks at the Palladium. In the US, the band played some small clubs in cities such as Dallas, Philadelphia and New York, but the practicality of working a band which had two bases some 6000 miles apart was non-existent. For the production of the album, Bruce Botnick returned to the fold, but it was a somewhat roundabout affair with the Olympic sessions engineered by Keith Harwood, the band then taking the tapes to Dynamic Sounds in Jamaica, where Bruce engineered the later sessions. Then everyone flew to Los Angeles where the album was mixed at Hollywood Sound. John recalls

"The English sessions took about three weeks, then three weeks in Jamaica and on to LA for the mixing, so the whole thing took maybe two months, and it was pretty much a continuous period."

Ray, in the meantime, hadn't been idle since the disintegration of the Doors. Having flown back to the States, one of his first moves was to enter into a managerial partnership with one Danny Sugerman, who had been a Doors hanger-on since the age of thirteen when, through his friend who was

then the Doors roadie, he'd met and fallen under the spell of Jim Morrison. Since that time, he'd become accepted as an integral – if minor – cog in the Doors machinery. Whilst Ray and Danny were in pursuit of a record deal, Elektra Records shuffled the Doors back catalogue one more time, dealing out the strangest compilation yet. Aside from a demonstrably inaccurate title, *The Best Of The Doors* (which it most certainly was not) contained tracks taken from all the albums bar *Morrison Hotel*, all remastered to produce a quadrophonic mix – a questionable move for several reasons. Firstly, around 1973 it was becoming obvious that quad was *not* going to be the next big audio advance, as had been predicted, and therefore relatively few people possessed the hardware; two, in the remastering process, something had gone awry and, when heard in stereo or mono, the bass end appeared to have vanished; and three, the quadrophonic reproduction isn't the highest of fi. However, such was the loyalty of the die-hards and completists that the album crept into the charts for a few weeks, peaking at 158.

Ray eventually secured his own deal with Mercury Records and in 1974 released two solo records. Following the break-up of the Doors, John had noted that,

"I think Ray's going to take off where the Doors left off, with your mystical piano playing...",

a point the first Manzarek effort confirmed. *The Golden Scarab* (subtitled *A Rhythm Myth*), boasting titles such as *The Rumour Of Existence*, took as loose base the deities of ancient Egypt, but the music was firmly based in the late 20th century jazz fusion field. As with *Full Circle*, perhaps the most noteworthy aspect of the album wasn't the music but the sleeve photos, which easily make the album cover one of the most repellent ever conceived (no reflection on Ray, but it's difficult to look one's best under gold full-face makeup). The overall musical impression is that of the ramblings of the final Doors LP carried one step further, to the stage where it becomes little more than background listening.

Between albums, Ray loaned his expertise

at the keyboard to Iggy Pop for his *Death Of Glitter* gig at the L.A. Palladium; other members of the pick-up band backing the Ig were Michael Des Barres, James Williamson (a former Stooge), Gary Mallaber (Steve Miller's drummer) and Nigel Harrison (ex of the late and singularly unlamented Silverhead, as was Des Barres), the latter two deciding to stay on with Ray and lend a hand on his second solo album, a set which also featured the ubiquitous Flo and Eddie, and Joe Walsh contributing some excellent guitar. *The Whole Thing Started With Rock & Roll, Now It's Out Of Control* was a distinct improvement on *The Golden Scarab*, the title track in particular being noteworthy, as was the instrumental *Whirling Dervish*. *I Wake Up Screaming* featured not only a very Doors-like opening but also one of the first appearances on disc of Patti Smith, intoning a poem from *The New Creatures*. Perhaps the most interesting track, both musically and lyrically, was the album's closing item, *Perfumed Garden*. Melodically, it resembled *The Peking King And The New York Queen* with rather more bite; lyrically, it was definitely X-rated, apparently taking its inspiration from the book of the same name. Suffice to say that the mid-song climax isn't restricted to the music and effectively quashed any hope of airplay! Nevertheless, enough people got to hear of the LP and like it to push it into the 150th slot in the charts.

Meanwhile, back with Robbie, John and the Butts Band, all was not well. The English contingent – Roden, Davies and Chen – had returned to the UK, and when John and Robbie travelled over, it was evident that the band couldn't stay together. As John outlined some two years later:

> "The trouble was that we really weren't together as a group. People were talking about solo albums, and it takes years to establish the foundation… it's a commitment, like being married. Four or five people have to say, 'OK, it's us against the world, we're gonna do it for three years or so, and then if nothing's happening we can think about solo projects.' That's what got me fed up, the lack of commitment."

108 Robbie was a little more diplomatic in his reflections on the break up of the first Butts Band;

> "We'd found some of the best musicians in Europe but, since John and I live in Los Angeles, it turned out to be imposssible to hold a group with two home bases together."

Jess Roden, reflecting on his time in the Butts Band, offers the following thoughts:

> "There was no 'ex-Doors' hype, and Robbie and John were both lovely people, with a genuine yearning to go back and start it all again without Jim, but for some reason, they didn't have the energy. We didn't have a lot in common, and what I found was that Jim had been such a powerful character for so long that they had no real strength to pursue a musical concept of their own… so we hardly did anything – a few clubs in the States, a nice scene but nothing special. We could have done it, either in the UK or USA, but it wasn't going anywhere… they didn't have to do IT again… not with the Butts Band anyway."

John and Robbie then returned to Los Angeles and began checking out possible members for a new Butts Band. By November, the second incarnation of the Butts Band was ready. Sharing the drum stool with John was Mike Zorkowitz whilst completing the rhythm section was Carl 'Slick' Rucker, a veteran R&B session and tour player, having backed up the likes of Ike & Tina Turner and the Chi-Lites. Keyboard and vocal duties were handled by Alexandra Richman, formerly a solo artist with Capitol. As the vocalist (and occasional guitarist and pianist), Mike Stull had been involved with the Doors some three years earlier, when his then band, the Wackers, opened for them at Carnegie Hall. Unofficially completing the line-up was Bobbi Hall on congas, who had worked on the *Full Circle* sessions. The resultant album, *Hear And Now!* (released in early 1975) was remarkably similar to *The Butts Band* in that it broke no new ground and further showcased Robbie's ever-excellent guitar. In fact, it was only Robbie's breaks that saved some of the tracks from total mediocrity. Just two cuts caught the ear, the opening *Get Up*,

Stand Up (the Bob Marley song) because of its incongruity, and *Caught In The Middle*, for its Morrisonesque midsong rap. Otherwise, the tracks were perfectly suited to the cocktail lounge circuit and the album accordingly caused as little commotion in the music world as the second Butts Band. Though possessed of a more stable geographical base, there was apparently still a certain lack of commitment; thus, following the release of *Hear And Now!* the future of the Butts Band seemed uncertain.

With Ray maintaining a discreetly low profile throughout 1975, the only other news on the Doors front was that a film soundtrack composed entirely of Doors recordings was being considered by director Francis Ford Coppola for his upcoming Vietnam epic, *Apocalypse Now*. Towards the end of the year, Coppola abandoned the idea and approached Ray, whom he'd known at UCLA film school (and therefore Jim as well, one assumes), to compose a score for the film utilising Door riffs and song fragments. As Jim had proved, Doors plus film usually equates with inaction and, for various reasons, that's exactly what happened. This, however, is anticipating events somewhat... It wasn't too far into 1976 before the Butts Band folded completely and the experience apparently decided John that the world of rock could get along without him quite nicely, whereupon he proceeded to head off in a totally different direction, that of acting.

> *"I'm not bitter, it's not that music has disillusioned me... but it's hard to find the right people and make something as special as we had going with the Doors. Anyway, I went and saw my father in a play. He used to act when he was my age, and then about forty years later he goes back on the boards. It was like seeing a completely different person on stage, somebody I didn't know at all, and I thought 'Hey, this is interesting!'"*

Thus inspired John wasted little time enrolling in various drama workshops and classes, generally immersing himself in his chosen new field with commendable enthusiasm.

Ray, following a largely quiet 1975, was in the process of putting a new band together –

the *Apocalypse Now* project hadn't been completely abandoned but it was becoming evident that it was unlikely to happen – utilising new L.A. musicians influenced by the British punk/new wave explosion, news of which was beginning to filter back to the West Coast. Bassman Nigel Harrison from *The Whole Thing...* had kept in touch with Ray and was naturally in the band, known as Nite City, along with previous unknowns Jimmy Hunter (vocals and drums), Paul Warren (vocals and guitar) and Noah James (vocals). Due in no small part to Danny Sugerman's enthusiastic management, the band quickly landed a deal with 20th Century Records and began recording their debut set.

Robbie meanwhile, had similarly secured a deal with the Blue Note label and was recording what John labels

> "*A jazz fusion/funk-rock album which was pretty progressive. I actually played on a little of it; one cut, that's all – I didn't want to do the whole thing*",

and when the album was entering the final stages – sweetening and the like – was struck by an idle thought:

> "*I just happened to be thinking about the poetry Jim had recorded about five years back – I suppose someone must have mentioned it to me or something – so I called up John Haeny, who'd engineered the sessions and said 'Whatever happened to Jim's poetry tapes? Do you have any copies?' The guy said, 'Better than that, I've got the originals – why don't you and the other guys come over, we can listen to them, see if there's anything there, and maybe we can do something with them.' And that's how it all got started.*"

One wonders whether, if the effort eventually required to complete the project had been made obvious to the band at the time, the project would have materialised.

The early months of 1977 saw the release of both *Robbie Krieger And Friends* and the eponymous first album from Nite City. Nite City has more recently been considered amongst the precursors of West Coast new wave, but on the whole *Nite City* was a slightly more polished set than what followed. Of the nine songs (including one instrumental by Ray which would have fitted perfectly on *The Golden Scarab*), the most interesting – though not in strictly musical terms - was *Angel w/ No Freedom*, a track which immediately attracted the attention of Morrison fanatics as a possible clue to Jim's death. Admittedly, the lyric is sufficiently vague to allow such an interpretation, with reference to a "wild child" and the final line, "Heroin killed my best friend" supplying apparent confirmation of the most widely accepted 'means of death' rumour, but the overall impression is either of some wishful thinking on the fans' behalf, or someone having a somewhat cheap joke – and with Ray and Danny Sugerman involved, the latter seems most improbable. The album aroused interest in the L.A. area but did little on a national basis; vocalist Noah James departed the scene and the remaining quartet recorded a second album, *Golden Days And Diamond Nights*, before disbanding in late 1977. Nigel Harrison moved on to join Blondie just as they were beginning to break, a slice of good luck if there ever was one. The second album didn't see the light of day until early 1979 due, according to Ray, to internal complications with the record company -

> "*the president was fired, everything was restructured and somehow the album got lost in the shuffle.*"

Well, not quite lost completely, but to the extent that it was released only in West Germany.

Robbie's album was exactly as John described it, jazz rock with a touch of funk – an excellent showcase for Mr. Krieger's guitar talents, but hardly compulsive listening unless your idea of heaven is Chick Corea or Weather Report. Perfect cruising music...

Inevitably, word that the legendary Morrison poetry tapes might soon see the light of day, or that at least, some form of genuinely new Doors product was forthcoming, leaked out, arousing great expectations – somewhat prematurely as it happened. In the summer of 1977, John gave the rumours a solid base, at the same time hinting that it wasn't going to be as easy as they'd first thought.

"We've been researching these damned poems for about a year or so, but the last few months we've been getting serious, meeting a couple of times a week. Hopefully, in the next two or three months, we'll get into it five days a week, wrap it up and have it out for Christmas but... you see, this is our *idea. It's not one of your Jimi Hendrix fourth album after he's died thing, jamming in the background with some fat jazz sax player, nor is it a case of the record company going back into the files, digging out some old tapes and putting them out with a new jacket. This is Jim's poetry album – he never got to finish it, so now Ray, Robbie and I are doing it for him. It's not going to be a straight blah, blah, blah, nothing straight through for ten*

8

*minutes or whatever. It's going to be like a
biography; his childhood, teenage years,
young man, public life. It was all done on
a 16-track, so we're gonna write some new
music under the poems, and we'll have a
little bit of old stuff to tie it all together,
plus some real nice stories he tells about
when he was making his films, various
things in his life. They make it kinda
biographical, and so it has a little theme.
It's Jim's life, really."*

In the course of the same interview, the
subject of a currently circulating rumour was
mentioned, to wit, that as graves in France
are apparently rented, Jim's resting place was
due for renewal, failing which the coffin
would be disinterred and re-buried in a
collective plot; John was able to comment on
this.

*"Well... I know a little. I read that story
and the outcome was that Ray, Robbie
and I gave some money to have the grave
taken care of. It was quite a considerable
sum, and should have been enough to make
sure that everything was taken care of, but
somebody made off with it... I don't want
to say who, one of his close relatives or*

114

whatever, but that's the story on the grave. We tried..."

As it happens, the rumour seems to have been unfounded, for there is no evidence of Jim's alleged grave having been opened.

John's slight reservation at naming a definite release date for the album was justified as Christmas 1977 came and went with no appearance of "The Morrison Project", as it had rapidly become known.

"We ran into snags"
said Ray at the album's eventual release, Robbie clarifying

"The fact is that this album is so revolutionary in the way we had to make it that we really shouldn't have projected dates. There was no way to tell how long something was going to take... it turned out that for everything we said 'OK, this shouldn't take more than a month', it took about three months."

"We had no models to work from,"
concluded Ray *"because a record like this had never been made before."*

An American Prayer, credited to Jim Morrison with "music by the Doors", was finally released in November 1978, taking its title from the album's major poetic extract, the only previously published material and a selection almost dictated by public demand. Ray:

"An American Prayer was a private edition that Jim handed out to friends and certain fans, and in the past seven years, I've had many people come up to me and say. 'How do I get a copy of it? I've heard of it and I want to read it.' So, naturally, we thought it would have to be included on the album. It was so good, we felt it belonged in a larger scope than just 500 copies out there somewhere."

The process of recording the new musical pieces behind Jim's poetry, as related by Ray, differs from the way the Doors had always pieced together their songs in one detail only. This time, there was no way Jim could be persuaded to change the style or pacing of any of his contributions in order to fit the music.

"Jim was getting back at us" was John's view of the sessions. *"This time, it's like he's saying. 'OK, now it's your turn to do the overdubs!'"*

Ray considers that

"Jim always had a sense of implied rhythm in his poems, so consequently it was pretty easy for us, as musicians, to lock into a rhythm one way or another... So, when we heard the poetry, we said, 'OK, here's this implied rhythm – let's just make it explicit.' Ghost Song, for example; in the end Jim gets to talking about the dead Indians on the highway, so we knew that required an Indian beat. So, John got started off on the drums with this tom-tom beat, and from that I put in an Em^7 / Em^9 on top, feeling the same rhythm. Robbie started on his guitar, a couple of little licks and lines, and then on top of that we just put Jim's poetry; we spaced it out a little bit, made a few cuts here and there, kinda 'wait Jim, wait four bars and let us play this little line, then you can come back in again.' It was almost like working with the man in person... it was a very eerie feeling, because Jim was really there at rehearsals. It was the three of us and Jim on tape. OK, so he wasn't there in person, but his presence was almost tangible. Recording the new stuff took about two months..."

If this is so, then more than a few people must've wondered why *An American Prayer* took so very long to hit the stores: the new backing tracks are supplemented by snatches of old Doors records and actually account for only slightly more than half of the album. Subsequent listenings reveal the reason for the album's delay – the painstaking and almost infinite care with which the project was pieced together. Considering the various ages and condition of the masters used, it's a positive compliment that there is only the one obvious edit – and that's in the track Jim provided! Where new Doors material segues into old, it is genuinely a case of not being able to hear the join.

Ray had just one reservation concerning *An American Prayer*:

"I hope the audience, the people who are going to listen to this album, will perceive that it's a quite unique experience... it's not something to put on while you're doing the

dishes, or mending the car. You have to put this record on, sit down and listen. It demands... all it asks for is forty minutes of your time; and if you give us those forty minutes, we'll take you somewhere that you've maybe never been before..."

Unlike many, if not most, spoken word/ poetry recordings, *An American Prayer* stands repeated listening – not simply once every three months or so, but three, four, five times in succession, for there's always something new to pick up on, even if it is only trying to work out exactly what *is* going on behind *The World On Fire* (Anti-war demonstration? Riot at a Doors concert?). The most important aspect of the album is not that a legend of rock was finally released (and was seen to be equal to its reputation, something Spirit's *Potatoland* opus fell somewhat short of, leaving the Beach Boys' *Smile* as the undisputed Mythical Rock Artifact) but that it showcased the poetry of Jim Morrison in its most apposite context, that of performance. As previously noted, the cold print of *The New Creatures* reflected little apparent credit on Jim's ability as a poet – nor, indeed, does the text of the booklet included in the album package. But actually hearing Jim declaim the same lines adds not only the dimension of performance, but also that of Jim's presence, the missing ingredient of all post-Paris Doors releases. It was obvious that, even through the medium (no pun intended) of recording tape and the studio, the 'old' Doors chemistry was bubbling again, the backing perfectly complementing the 'lyric'. The choice of using selected cuts from the Doors back catalogue never fails to work and is, on occasion, inspired – the juxtaposition of *Riders On The Storm* with what appears to be a segment of the *HWY* movie, the linking of *Ghost Song* with *Newborn Awakening* via a snatch of *Peace Frog*.

The new musical fragments, though ostensibly composed to fit with the rhythm and mood of the verse, would appear to owe more to *Other Voices* and *Full Circle* than, say, *Morrison Hotel* or *L.A. Woman*, that is rather more jazzy than your average Doors fare, and would seem to indicate that, had

Jim hung around a while longer, the Doors would still be functioning, or at the very least, that their final two albums wouldn't have been as average as they turned out.

The point on which *An American Prayer* stands or falls, however, is Jim's verse, all previously unpublished apart from the title track, and in the main, it is a great improvement over previously available material. Not that there aren't any dubious tracks; *The Movie* suffers principally from suspect engineering and production, resulting in gimmicky cross-speaker talk, whilst *Lament (For My Cock)* sports not only an incongruous backing track but a theme and treatment which embarrass, not because of the content but because of the surprising ineptitude and unabashed vulgarity the piece displays.

A bonus for the more musically-oriented Doors fan was the inclusion of a live *Roadhouse Blues*, so very fine that one wonders why it is omitted from *Absolutely Live*. Robbie recalls the reason being that

> *"It came out on the album right before we started doing the live one, so we figured, 'Well, we've just done this one so we can't really put out a live version right now.'"*

Ray attributed its inclusion to

> *"needing something for the 'public life' part, so we listened to all the live out-takes and we found about six or seven takes of* Roadhouse Blues *just lying there, waiting for the right time to come out."*

There was almost another live bonus, in the form of the old Them standard *Gloria*, but for no known reason, it was dropped from the album. Robbie attempted an explanation:

> *"There was another thing; we were going to use* Gloria *but we had some problems amongst ourselves as to, you know, whether or not to use it, because...'*

at which point the conversation broke off then turned to other matters.

Ray's concern that the record-buying public might not be able to relate to the album proved groundless as it rapidly reached fifty-four in the American charts – perhaps not so good in the light of previous Doors releases, but almost unprecedented for an essentially spoken word album – a rating which could well have been improved upon were it not for the confusion the album caused with radio programmers, who didn't apparently have the least idea how to present it. In one of the odder episodes of Doors' history, Elektra produced a special radio-play edition, which had *Lament*, *The Movie*, *Angels And Sailors* and *Curses, Invocations* deleted completely, whilst *Black Polished Chrome* and *An American Prayer* itself underwent minor surgery. The reviews of the album were, almost without exception, extremely favourable. However, one dissenting voice hailed from an unexpected quarter: *"That album was a rape"* declared Paul Rothchild.

"In my mind, what they did to An American Prayer *was on a par with taking a painting by Picasso, cutting it up into hundreds of small pieces and spreading it across a supermarket wall. It was the first commercial sell-out of Jim Morrison."*

Whilst Rothchild's observation may be slightly exaggerated, there is an element of truth in it, for whilst it was Jim performing his own verse, the end product was constructed by people who, although close associates of the man, couldn't possibly have had even the slightest notion of how Jim would have utilised the same material. In this aspect, *An American Prayer* does have a counterpart – the songs released after the death of Buddy Holly consisting of Holly's demos or basic tracks with full arrangements dubbed over them. Equally, *An American Prayer* utilised less than one tenth of the poetry material known to have been recorded, which raises either hopes of further vol umes in the series... or suspicions that Ray, Robbie, John and Frank Lisciandro have executed one of the best cover-ups since Watergate, and that the majority of the legendary Morrison poetry tapes are, in fact, significantly less than wonderful as regards content... In an interview to promote the poetry album, Ray intimated that it was a one-off, and that the next project would be visual rather than aural:

"We have 50,000 feet or so of footage of the Doors. That's lurking in the wings, *very possibly one of the next projects... but the reason why it's lurking is that, like this album, if it's done, it's going to be done properly."*

One project definitely *not* in the works, media and industry rumours notwithstanding, was a Doors reunion on a permanent and performing basis, as John was quick to point out:

"Just a rumour, nothing more. We've seen the press clippings and had a good laugh..."

Rather than cash in on their new found (albeit reflected) fame and fortune, Ray, John and Robbie simply went back to what they were doing before and during the making of the album. John returned to his acting workshops and classes, though managing to keep his drumming hand in by contributing percussion to Beth Snyder's Dance Company production in the spring of 1980. In 1981, he embarked on his first true steps in his new chosen profession with a guest spot in several episodes of one of the most popular American soap operas, *One Day At A Time* (which also featured Mackenzie Phillips, daughter of John Phillips of The Mamas & Papas).

Robbie similarly picked up the threads of his solo career, though not for very long:

"I planned to do another album like the Blue Note one, but then I started getting interested in this new wave stuff. I'd met this singer from England, Mac Mackenzie, who'd done some work with the Gang of Four. He'd got some good material, so I thought I'd produce him and we went into a studio and cut some tracks... then a friend of mine who worked on An American Prayer, *Arthur Barrow, got fired from Frank Zappa's band, called me and said, 'I've been wanting to get into this new wave thing', and I said 'Well, I have this guy...' so we got together."*

Getting together entailed the formation, in August 1980, of Red Shift, a "new wave band with Zappa and jazz influences" (according to Robbie) who played the L.A. clubs, cut further demo tapes and went into stasis after a few months when Mackenzie returned to the UK and Barrow was re-admitted to the

Zappa fold. The story doesn't end there, but events are beginning to get ahead of themselves a touch...

One of the most eagerly anticipated films of 1979 was Francis Ford Coppola's statement on Vietnam, *Apocalypse Now*. Though the idea of having Ray compose a score had long fallen by the wayside, Coppola was determined to have the Doors represented in the film somehow, as they were apparently the listeners' choice amongst those doing their patriotic duty. After shooting and discarding a sequence in which Kurtz (Marlon Brando) teaches his private army of local tribesmen the lyric and general rhythm of *Light My Fire* (in their own dialect!), Coppola settled for opening and closing the movie with *The End* remixed to bring up a vocal part which Rothchild, in the original track, felt he had to mix down to the threshold of inaudibility.

> *"During the whole big raga thing, Jim's going 'kill, kill, kill', and at another point he's going 'fuck, fuck, fuck' as a rhythm instrument..."*

Interestingly both *An American Prayer* and the *Apocalypse Now* soundtrack LP were nominated for Grammy awards in the Best Spoken Word category but neither won.

Ray, in the meantime hadn't been idle; as with Robbie, he'd become interested in the LA new wave scene and was often to be found in the unlikeliest venues checking out emerging talent. He was, in fact, the earliest of the music biz 'figures' to jam with the Knack, a tag of dubious merit these days but back then, reasonably hip. In the fall of 1979, Ray and Danny Sugerman formed New Way Productions, and at once began working with two of the most talked about new wave bands in Los Angeles, the Zippers and X.

> *"Both X and the Zippers have the intensity in their music that I look for. They come from different ends of the musical spectrum, but they share common ground in their attitude, which is 'We gotta get out of this place'".*

The first fruit of Ray's headlong plunge into new wave saw daylight in April 1980, with the release of *Los Angeles*, the debut album from X. Comprising Exene Cervenka (vocals), Don J. Bonebrake (drums), Billy Zoom (guitar) and John Doe (bass, vocals and no relation), X had been together since late 1977, but it seemed that Ray was to be their catalyst. *Los Angeles* was accorded rave reviews, was voted the best album of the year by the L.A. Times and turned out to be the best selling independent release (on Slash Records) in America that year. Not bad for an album recorded in three weeks on a budget of $10,000... but was all the fuss justified? Applied to a band that made the early Sex Pistols sound positively polished, phrases such as "...troubled sketches of people pushing themselves to emotional limits" and "...essence of Hollywood Babylon" seem, at best, pretentious. A more accurate description hailed their sound as "raw, frenzied, uncompromising punk", which is far nearer the mark; had this album been issued in the UK in, say, 1977, nary an eyebrow would have elevated. Issuing as it did from Los Angeles in the first year of the eighties, it was something to be noted. Aside from the personnel mentioned, Ray himself stepped out from the production cubicle and contributed some organ overdubs... though not, apparently, on *Soul Kitchen*, probably the most unorthodox cover of a Doors song to date. A lyric sheet was included in the album package, it might be unkindly thought out of necessity, as the majority of the lyrics on the disc were somewhat indecipherable to the average record buyer.

In January 1980, Robbie also put together a production company, Line Productions and began working with the Willys, another L.A. club act. To date, the union has proved less than abundantly fruitful, being limited to one track – *She's Illegal* – on *Sharp Cuts*, a Planet compilation released in mid-1980.

However, beyond any shadow of a doubt the major Doors-related event of 1980 was the publication by Warner Books in June of the self-proclaimed long-awaited biography of Jim Morrison, *No One Here Gets Out Alive*, co-authored by Jerry Hopkins, with an acclaimed book on Presley to his credit, and Danny Sugerman, who took upon himself the task of assembling and editing the final manuscript from Hopkins' previous drafts, which had been turned down by at least one publisher as uncommercially lengthy. The commercial viability of the artefact that eventually appeared was swiftly established as the book soared to the top of the best-seller lists and stayed there for six weeks; by mid-1982, several million copies had been sold, proving, if nothing else, that the American reading public liked their rock stars excessive and dead (something Albert Goldman's *Elvis* would confirm the following year). The rock establishment tended, in the main, to take a different view; whilst never denying that the book contained a mass of new information, especially that concerning Jim's childhood and teenage years, there were distinct reservations concerning the veracity of certain portions (some of the conversations presented as fact *do*, in fact, come over as less than plausible) and the involvement of Sugerman (who crops up quite frequently in the text of the book under the none too subtle pseudonym of Denny Sullivan), a self-confessed Jim Morrison acolyte. Jac Holzman, when questioned, was concise and acid:

> *"The book was nothing but a repackaging job – not serious. It was too monumental, and tended to sensationalise aspects of Jim's character best ignored. The death rumours? Not only sick but unbelievable. Danny Sugerman – how can I phrase this tactfully – wasn't as tight with Jim as you'd think from the book... I doubt if anyone knew Jim that well."*

The general consensus of opinion in the rock press on the subject of *No One Here Gets Out Alive* walked a line between 'it's OK as far as it goes (which isn't really far enough)' and 'it'll do until the definitive volume comes along'. As noted above, the public took little if any note of the professional knockers, and purchased the book in droves, thus causing the Hollywood film industry to sit up and start making noises about a Jim Morrison film. One of the most vociferous proved to be John Travolta, announcing that he would be taking the lead role in any such venture. The cinematic side of the new resurgence of interest in the Doors swiftly resolved itself into two camps, each convinced of its own special merits. On one hand, the Warners project based – not unnaturally – on the Sugerman/Hopkins book, and on the other a project announced by a decidedly unexpected source, the Morrison family. Having already shown their antagonism towards anything connected with the book by refusing permission for any of Jim's poems to be fully quoted, the decision to make their own film must have surprised many, especially the pronouncement that

> *"the film will be the family's view, because what no-one knew is that towards the end of his life, Jim mellowed out and became close to his family again",*

according to Alan Graham (who married Jim's sister), who further added

> *"Warner Brothers were warned that if they make their movie, we'll sue them."*

For a family whom Jim studiously ignored for most of his adult life, an amazing degree of concern was suddenly being displayed...

October 1980 saw, almost inevitably given the boost of the book, yet another compilation, again with a less than accurate title. *The Doors Greatest Hits* suffered mainly from a limited back catalogue, which accounted for the inclusion of songs which had not only *not* been hits – *Roadhouse Blues* (live) – but hadn't even been issued as singles – *L.A. Woman* and *Not To Touch The Earth*. For reasons never adequately explained, all the tracks were re-mastered, with much the same effect as was evident on the *Best Of The Doors* compilation, i.e. the bass end tended to vanish every now and then. Needless to say, the package moved units at high speed eventually joining every other Morrison-period Doors album in the platinum league.

In terms of product, 1981 was a relatively fallow year on the Doors and related front. In May, *Wild Gift*, the second X album, was released and surpassed the success of its predecessor, selling some 100,000 copies, garnering more rave reviews, firmly establishing X as *the* new L.A. band and arousing interest among the major labels. Ray's other act, the Zippers, were not exciting any interest and in June 1981 called it a day, leaving a six-track 'mini-LP' on local L.A. label Rhino Records as the only trace of their **121** passing. At more or less the same time, Ray renewed a friendship stretching back to the Whiskey days when he approached Bryan Maclean, formerly of Love, with a view to producing Maclean's sister, Maria,

"He was only interested in Maria, so that was why we never really got any further than talking"

Maclean explains.

"He wanted me to step out of the way and let my sister be the band, but I wouldn't do it... but he's waiting – we didn't break things, it's just a big pause... It's gonna happen."

Robbie's production career, meanwhile, had joined Red Shift in limbo; no-one had picked up the Willys following the release of the *Sharp Cuts* sampler, and his most obvious effort of 1981 was a guest appearance on Blue Oyster Cult's *Extraterrestrial Live* double album (released in 1982), playing guitar on *Roadhouse Blues* at a December gig in Los Angeles. It would be nice to say that he contributed his usual excellent guitar, but the fact is that, of the several guitarists on the track, his own mother would be hard pressed to pick him out. And John just kept on with the classes...

As 1982 came round – for those who see significance in these things, the fifteenth anniversary of the first ever Doors release – there was more visible and potential activity in the Doors camp than there had been since the release of *An American Prayer*. The much vexed subject of films was still cropping up, and was still as puzzling as ever to the casual observer. The Morrison family film was slated to begin production in December, new Doors manager Ben Edmonds was seeking out live footage for a project combining actual archive material with documentary-style sequences and, just to complicate matters nicely, the completion of a film starring John Travolta as Jim was rumoured to have taken place...

Somewhat less convoluted was the vinyl scene. Red Shift gently folded, Arthur Barrow moving on to a band whose handle vacillated between the Acid Casualties and Panic Stations (finally settling for the for-

mer), who released an album, *Panic Station*, on Rhino Records which featured Robbie on four cuts of a set less new-wave than neo-psychedelic, as the covering of a Marc Bolan title and an obscure Pink Floyd single from the sixties testified. (By way of tying up ends, the majority of the new material on the album was co-authored by Daddy Maxfield, in fact, Graham Daddy and Louie Maxfield, one of whose '70s B sides had featured keyboards from one Ray Manzarek.)

The continued sucess of X – *Wild Gift* had sold over 100,000 copies – rang commercial bells in the offices of the major record labels, and to no-one's great surprise, they signed, ironically enough, with Elektra and in June released a third album (again with Ray producing), *Under The Big Black Sun*, which continued the musical direction of their previous albums, ensuring that if the true spirit of punk lived on anywhere, it was in the unlikely environs of Los Angeles. Not content with producing the biggest thing to come out of California for years, Ray cast an eye to the future and began producing a band tipped to be the Next Big Thing, Top Jimmy and the Rhythm Pigs... and in his spare time (or so it seems) began work on a third solo album, one which would make use of his classical piano training all those years ago in Chicago.

Robbie was likewise embarking on another solo project, a jazz-rock fusion album provisionally entitled *Mix* featuring Bruce Gary on drums, Don Preston (ex-Mother of Invention) on keyboards and a cameo appearance by one Mr Manzarek. On the production front, Robbie began working with Helena Springs, a former backing vocalist and songwriting crony of Bob Dylan.

John continued with his acting, making the odd appearance on TV, but also announced he was writing a book on his experiences during the Doors years, a volume not to be confused with the *Illustrated History of the Doors*, an 'in their own words' format scheduled for 1983. The eighties – or at least the early years thereof – would seem set to be awash with Morrison/Doors tomes, some of dubious worth. In 1982, three appeared; one, *Burn Down the Night* by Craig Strete, is in autobiographical form (as though written by Jim) and generally aroused much the same feelings among Doors fans as the previously mentioned Goldman book had evoked in Presley fans; a second, *Jim Morrison – An Hour For Magic* was written by ex-Morrison confidant Frank Lisciandro and consists of personal reminiscences – neither overly laudatory nor sensational, for once – plus several previously unpublished poems and a wealth of new photographs spanning the years 1968 to late 1970, making for a useful addition to the Doors fan's book shelf.

There have been rumours that 1982 will see a second Doors reunion on a more permanent basis than that required for the *American Prayer* sessions; at the time of writing, no confirmation or denial has been issued.

Following a summer of silence on the Doors front, the early fall of 1982 saw, if not exactly an explosion of news, then at least some interesting mentions in the gossip columns of the rock press. The topic of the Doors/Morrison film, already more than a little convoluted, took another twist with the announcement that William Friedkin, director of such noted movies as *The Exorcist* and *The French Connection* was being approached with an eye to making "... the definitive Doors movie." Whether this refers to Ben Edmonds' docu-drama style project or the Morrison family film is unclear. (On a more positive note, the rumoured Travolta-as-Jim film has yet to show its face in public, thus casting doubts as to whether it was completed or, indeed, ever commenced. Sighs of relief from all quarters...) An apparent off-shoot of the 'Family' film was revealed with the news that Jim's sister Anne had been auditioning Morrison lookalikes with the stated intent of staging a musical entitled *A Rock Saga – Jim Morrison Live*. The most intriguing aspect of this project was that it would reportedly be based on his biography which begs the question, is there yet another Morrison book in the offing? (It seems highly unlikely that a member of Jim's family would use the Sugerman/Hopkins book as a basis for such a project considering the lawsuits and brickbats they have hurled at it.) Also on the cinematic front, John continued to pursue his acting career with a role (size unspecified) in *Get Crazy*, a punk-comedy follow-up to *Rock & Roll Highschool*.

Easily the most interesting Doors news was that concerning the proposed spring 1983 release of an EP containing unreleased live tracks (presumably dating from the time of *Absolutely Live*); maybe the world will get to hear *Gloria* after all...

Or maybe not – neither the projected EP nor the *Illustrated History* appeared until close to the end of 1983, although Robbie did release his second solo LP, retitled *Versions*, since it now comprised instrumental cover versions plus a few Krieger originals. It was perhaps not sufficiently different from its predecessor to achieve major commercial success but a version of *The Crystal Ship* saw the three surviving Doors temporarily reunited. Robbie also played on a track of the comeback LP by the Honeys, an all girl trio including Brian Wilson's ex-wife Marilyn and her sister.

John was making distinct progress in the theatre, performing a pair of one man plays to considerable acclaim in Los Angeles – Sam Shepard's *Tongues* was linked with John's autobiographical one act play *Skins* (as in drums) to provide a solid evening's entertainment. Ray, of course, had several items on the go, among them a fourth LP by X, *More Fun In The New World*, which he once again produced. The album demonstrated the group's growing commercial viability, reaching the Top 100 in the US LP charts, although little musical change was audible. Ray was also working on a new solo project and turned up as a suprise guest on a cover version of *Riders On The Storm* by a young English ex-nurse, Annabel Lamb, which was a minor British hit. This resulted from working with A&M Records executive David Anderle on Manzarek's solo project – when Anderle enquired whether Ray might be interested in contributing to a second version of *Riders*, he accepted with alacrity. Even John and Robbie had a record released during the summer of 1983. As the Krieger-Densmore Reggae Bonanza, their 12" Rhino Records single coupled *Get Up, Stand Up* from the second Butts Band LP with a previously unreleased *Kinky Reggae* which

123

had been scheduled for release as a Butts Band single but was shelved when the band split up.

The fall of 1983 saw more Doors-related activity than for several years – Ray's solo project, a modern presentation of the classical piece by Carl Orff, *Carmina Burana*, produced by Philip Glass and featured synthesisers and an L.A. band, the Fents, was released and provoked much comment and interest, although this was apparently not reflected in sales. Perhaps it was just overshadowed by the October release of a new Doors album, *Alive She Cried*.

The original idea of a live EP had expanded after the arrival of a Danish video from the 1968 European tour containing a medley of *The WASP* and *Love Me Two Times*, which in its turn prompted an energetic search for tapes presumed to have been mislaid, which happily were soon discovered. The songs on the album span the years from 1968 to 1970, and include *Little Red Rooster* (with John Sebastion on harmonica) and even two of Jim's poems, inset into the breaks of two long tracks. *Gloria* did finally emerge, although what had been termed risqué earlier now seemed fairly normal, perhaps due to the song having been recorded at a soundcheck, and therefore lacking audience feedback. Completed by *Light My Fire*, *You Make Me Real* and *Moonlight Drive* (nothing from *Absolutely Live* was duplicated), *Alive She Cried* was an excellent coda to the previous live album although Robbie admitted that minor "improvements" had been undertaken and some errors corrected. That the joins are inaudible is to the credit of Paul Rothchild, who was reunited with 75% of the band with whom he had last worked thirteen years before.

Tieing in with the new LP was another addition to The Doors' bookshelf, Danny Sugerman's *Illustrated History Of The Doors* (perhaps a misleading credit, as 95% of the book consists of previously published press cuttings). However, the inclusion of many previously rare or unseen photographs of the band both individually and collectively more than made up for any overfamiliarity with parts of the text, and it hardly needs adding that both book and record sold in large quantities...

That the Doors music, name, legend and memory has persisted when so very many of their contemporaries have faded or fallen by the wayside is a tribute to the inherent qualities of the material and band members, as is their continued influence – how many other bands have had four admittedly obscure groups named after their songs? (L.A. Woman, Crystal Ship, Strange Daze and Moonlight Drive) – and popularity. Jim said it all back in 1965, when the Doors were as yet unformed and un-named; in response to Ray's desire to

> *"live to be 87 and see my great-grandchildren"*,

Jim stated

> *"Not me. I see myself... as a huge fiery comet, a shooting star. Everyone stops, points up and gasps 'Oh look at that!' Then – whoosh, and I'm gone... and they'll never see anything like it ever again... and they won't be able to forget me – ever."*

DOORS DISCOGRAPHY

(All releases both US and UK unless otherwise noted)

SINGLES:-

1/67 Break On Through/End Of The Night

4/67 Light My Fire/The Crystal Ship

5/67 Alabama Song/Take It As It Comes (UK)

9/67 People Are Strange/Unhappy Girl

11/67 Love Me Two Times/Moonlight Drive

3/68 The Unknown Soldier/We Could Be So Good Together

6/68 Hello, I Love You/Love Street

12/68 Touch Me/Wild Child

2/69 Wishful, Sinful/Who Scared You★

5/69 Tell All The People/Easy Ride

8/69 Running Blue/Do It (US)

3/70 You Make Me Real/Roadhouse Blues (double A side) (US)

4/70 You Make Me Real/The Spy (UK)

6/70 Roadhouse Blues/Blue Sunday (UK)

3/71 Love Her Madly/(You Need Meat) Don't Go No Further★

6/71 Riders On A Storm/Changeling

11/71 Tightrope Ride/Variety Is The Spice Of Life (US)

5/72 Ships W/ Sails/In The Eye Of The Sun (UK)

8/72 The Mosquito/It Slipped My Mind (US)

8/72 Get Up And Dance/Tree Trunks★★ (UK)

1/79 Roadhouse Blues (live)/Albinoni Adagio (US)

2/79 Roadhouse Blues (live)/Ghost Song (UK)

11/83 Gloria (live)/Love Me Two Times (live)

RE-ISSUES:-

4/71 Light My Fire/Love Me Two Times (US)

4/71 Touch Me/Hello, I Love You (US)

9/72 Riders On The Storm/Love Her Madly (US)

3/76 Riders On The Storm/L.A. Woman (UK)

6/76 Hello, I Love You/Love Me Two Times (UK)

8/80 Light My Fire/The Unknown Soldier (UK)

(The titles marked ★ were unavailable on album until the release of Weird Scenes Inside The Goldmine; *the title marked ★★ does not appear on any album.)*

ALBUMS:-

1/67 The Doors

10/67 Strange Days

7/68 Waiting For The Sun

7/69 The Soft Parade

2/70 Morrison Hotel

7/70 Absolutely Live (double)

11/70 13 (compilation)

4/71 L.A. Woman

11/71 Other Voices

1/72 Weird Scenes Inside The Goldmine (double compilation)

7/72 Full Circle

8/73 The Best Of The Doors (compilation)

11/78 An American Prayer

10/80 The Doors Greatest Hits (compilation)

10/83 Alive She Cried

(All the above titles released on the Elektra label)

ALBUMS FEATURING INDIVIDUAL MEMBERS OF THE DOORS:-

1974 Butts Band/Butts Band (Blue Thumb)

1974 The Golden Scarab/Ray Manzarek (Mercury)

1974 The Whole Thing Started With Rock & Roll, Now It's Out Of Control/Ray Manzarek (Mercury)

1975 Hear And Now!/Butts Band (Blue Thumb)

1975 For Real!/Jimi Hendrix (DJM - Jim (vocals & percussion) on one track, recorded 1970)

1977 Robbie Krieger & Friends (Blue Note - aside from the obvious, John drums on one track)

1977 Nite City /Nite City (20th Century - Ray)

1978 Golden Days & Diamond Nights/Nite City (released in West Germany only)

1980 Sharp Cuts/Various (Planet - sampler LP, Willys track co-produced by Robbie)

125

1980 Los Angeles/X (Slash - Ray produced and plays organ)

1980 Woke Up This Morning And Found Myself Dead/Jimi Hendrix (Red Lightnin' - recorded live at the Scene club, NY, in 1968; Jim credited with harmonica, vocals, abuse, obscenities, mumbling...)

1981 Wild Gift/X (Slash - Ray produced)

1981 The Zippers/The Zippers (Rhino - Ray produced)

1982 Extraterrestrial Live/Blue Oyster Cult (CBS - Robbie guests on one track)

1982 Panic Station/The Acid Casualties (Rhino - Robbie guests on four tracks)

1982 Under The Big Black Sun/X (Electra - Ray produced)

1983 Versions/Robbie Krieger (Passport (US)/ Shanghai (UK) - Ray & John guest on one cut)

1983 Ecstasy/Honeys (Rhino - Robbie guests on one track)

1983 More Fun In The New World/X (Elektra - Ray produced)

1983 Carmina Burana/Ray Manzarek (A&M)

(A few oddities that don't fit anywhere else: a section of The End *was released as an Electra 45 A side to coincide with the* Apocalypse Now *film... Ray played a mellotron string ensemble on a late seventies B side by Daddy Maxfield on Rhino... and Robbie & John produced an album for The Comfortable Chair on Ode in the mid-seventies, but no exact date can be confirmed. The album* - The Comfortable Chair - *is pretty dire... Rhino released two Butts Band tracks - one previously unreleased - on a 12" single under the banner of the Densmore-Krieger Reggae Bonanza... and Ray played keyboards on Annabel Lamb's cover version of* Riders On The Storm...)

BOOTLEGS:-

The dates ascribed to the following records refer more to the date recorded than to the actual date of "release" (which is almost impossible to pin down anyway...).

1967 Moonlight Drive (Live at the Matrix, San Francisco - also known as Weird Triangle) - *recorded in two track stereo before an apparent crowd of three, the album contains one as yet unreleased blues dirge,* Get Off My Life.
Side One:- People Are Strange/Alabama Song/Crystal Ship/Unhappy Girl/Moonlight

Drive/Summer's Almost Gone
Side Two:- Twentieth Century Fox/Back Door Man/My Eyes Have Seen You/Soul Kitchen/Get Off My Life/Crawling King Snake

1968 The Lizard King (live at the Roundhouse, London) - *a reasonable quality audience tape, which is* not *stereo, contrary to what the sleeve might claim.*
Side One:- Light My Fire/The End
Side Two:- Five To One/Break On Through/ When The Music's Over

1968/ Resurrection (*double set, tagged* French Fan
69 Club Release) - *in the main, material from the European tour of 1968, with a few odd tracks of interest.*
Side One:- When The Music's Over/Five To One/Spanish Caravan
Side Two:- Back Door Man-Crawling King Snake/Celebration Of The Lizard (excerpt)- Light My Fire/Unknown Soldier (*both sides are live at the Roundhouse, recorded from the TV special "The Doors Are Open" - not the same show as "The Lizard King")*
Side Three:- Celebration Of The Lizard (excerpt) - Light My Fire/Five To One/Love Me Two Times
Side Four:- Mack The Knife-Alabama Song-Back Door Man/Moonlight Drive/Light My Fire/Who Do You Love/Miami Rap excerpts (*side three and first track on side four recorded in Stockholm 1968, tracks two and three from the Jonathon Winters TV Show 1967, track four at the Matrix 1967. The less said about track five the better...)*

1968/ Mr. Mojo Risin' (double set) - *late sixties TV*
69 *and film material.*
Side One:- Opening dialogue/Wild Child/ Moonlight Drive/Jim backstage with pastor/ Five To One/Not To Touch The Earth/ Backstage dialogue/Airplane poem/Jim improvising with piano
Side Two:- The End/Closing Theme/Jim's comments on 'Feast Of Friends' (*sides one and two are the complete* Feast Of Friends *soundtrack)*
Side Three:- Light My Fire (Sullivan Show 1967)/The End
Side Four:- Wild Child/Touch Me (both from Smothers Brothers Show 1968)/ Interview for 'Critique' PBS show, 1969

1968/ Critique - *more late sixties TV material.*
69 Side One:- Tell All The People/Alabama Song-Back Door Man/Wishful, Sinful/Build

Me A Woman
Side Two:- The Soft Parade-Five To One/
Interview/Light My Fire/The Unknown
Soldier (*last two tracks on side two from 1968
Roundhouse TV show, all others from the 1969
'Critique' PBS show*)

1965/ Celebration (double set) - *mostly live material*
70 *which, label notwithstanding, is largely in
mono, and pretty poor quality at that.*
Side One:- Intro/Moonlight Drive*/Hello, I
Love You*/Summer's Almost Gone*/My
Eyes Have Seen You*/End Of The Night*/
Not To Touch The Earth*/Crystal Ship/
Alabama Song/Back Door Man/Five To One
Side Two:- Intro 2/Roadhouse Blues/Ship Of
Fools/Universal Mind/Money/Louie Louie/
Heartbreak Motel/Fever-Summertime-Easy
Ride-St. James Infirmary-Fire
Side Three:- Get Off My Life Woman/
Crawling King Snake/I Can't See Your
Face/The End
Side Four:- Changeling/L.A. Woman

(*The asterisked tracks on side one are the
September 1965 Aura session demos, the band
at the time being Jim, Ray, John, Rick & Jim
Manzarek and a mystery female bassist. The
remainder of side one is live, location unknown
and recorded after Miama, if Jim's comments
are any indication. Side two up to* Money *is live
in New York, either late 1969 or - more likely -
early 1970. Where the remainder was taped is
anyone's guess - the only certain factor is that the
quality is terrible. All of side three bar* The End
is from the Matrix, *1967, though* I Can't See
Your Face *hasn't appeared on a bootleg before.*
The End *is taken from the* Lizard King *LP.
Side four was recorded December 11th, 1970 in
Dallas. The actual packaging is good - gatefold
with colour & b/w shots - but confusing.* Hello,
I Love You *isn't listed,* Fire (*as in* Light My
…) *appears as a snippet at the beginning of side
four and the labels of sides two and three are
transposed. There are no liner notes, hence the
uncertainty as regards dates and locations.*)

The Moonlight Drive *LP has a plain yellow label
bearing the words 'side one' and 'side two'. Though it
means next to nothing, the others boast the following
'labels':*

The Lizard King - Round LIZLP 1968
Resurrection - Paris Records 7-3-71
Mr. Mojo Risin' - Towne Records K 413
Critique - Deja Vu Records D-1985
Celebration - Z1909/Z2010

In 1979, there appeared Apocalypse Now, *on Tuna
Records 213, which is either a reissue or a rip-off of*
The Lizard King. *Be warned…*

Bibliography:-

1969 Jim Morrison & The Doors - An
Unauthorised Book (Mike Jahn, Grosset &
Dunlap)

1969 The Lords/Notes On Vision (Jim Morrison,
private edition of 100)

1969 The New Creatures (Jim Morrison, private
edition of 100)

1970 The Lords & The New Creatures (Jim
Morrison, Simon & Schuster)

1970 An American Prayer (Jim Morrison, private
edition of 500)

1971 The Lords & The New Creatures
(paperback edition)

1980 No One Here Gets Out Alive (Jerry Hopkins
& Danny Sugerman, Warner Books (US),
Plexus (UK))

1982 Jim Morrison - An Hour For Magic (Frank
Lisciandro, Delilah Books (US), Eel Pie
(UK))

1982 Burn Down The Night (Craig Kee Strete,
Random House (US only))

1983 The Illustrated History Of The Doors
(Danny Sugerman, Quill (US), Vermilion
(UK))

Filmography:-

1967 Break On Through promo (*colour*)

1968 The Unknown Soldier promo (*colour*)

1968 Feast Of Friends documentary (*colour with
some black & white footage - all music is
pre-recorded; 40 minutes*)

1968 HWY (*colour; 50 minutes*)

1968 The Doors Are Open (*black & white
videotape of live footage at the London
Roundhouse - with live sound - spliced with
footage of 1968 political events; 60 minutes*)

1980 No One Here Gets Out Alive (*colour
videotape of live footage from* Feast Of
Friends, *and various US TV shows, also some
b & w Roundhouse footage - plus interviews
with John, Robbie, Ray, Rothchild, Hopkins,
Sugerman & footage of Jim.*)

127